Acknowledgements

This review was prepared as part of the background to a larger research project concerned with evaluating support for informal carers. This, and its companion review, *Families Caring for a Person Diagnosed as Mentally Ill: The Literature Re-examined*, by C. Perring, J. Twigg and K. Atkin, form the first publications of the project. The major empirical part of the research is due to be completed in 1990; and it is intended that its conclusions will be published in a series of papers, articles and publications during 1990 and 1991.

The project had been undertaken at the Social Policy Research Unit, University of York, and has been funded by the Department of Health. It forms part of a programme of work on informal care undertaken at the unit. Other publications in this field will appear as part of this HMSO/SPRU series. We would like to thank our many colleagues at SPRU for their helpful comments and suggestions. Particular thanks go to Gillian Parker and Patricia Thornton.

Contents

PART ONE

The scope of the subject

Introduction

Over the last decade, the subject of informal care has increasingly been in the forefront of policy. There are a number of reasons for this,. Concern over demographic change has raised the spectre of rising numbers of elderly people, and provoked anxiety over the consequent dependency ratio between the frail and the able bodied in society. This anxiety has been expressed both in terms of the actual cost of supporting people and in terms of the availability of direct family support. Changes in family patterns brought about by divorce and the growth of co-habitation have added further elements of uncertainty, as has the growing expectation of women to be able to participate fully in the labour market. These issues are explored in detail by Finch (1989) who has reviewed the current state of the literature in relation to family obligation and changing social structures.

Changes in perceptions and ideology have also been significant in creating concern over the issue of informal care. A major thrust behind the development of the subject both academically and in public consciousness has come from the feminist critique. This has been concerned to expose the gendered nature of informal care and, with it, the potentially exploitative character of community care policy. A stream of work has developed and refined these ideas over the last decade (Finch and Groves 1982, Wilson 1982, Ungerson 1987, Finch 1987, Baldwin and Twigg 1990). From a diametrically opposed viewpoint has come the second major influence in the debate: that of conservative and neo-liberal social and political thought which emphasises the family caring for its own and seeks to encourage informal caring as opposed to that of statutory bodies. This ideological preference is closely linked to economic and fiscal arguments.

As a result of these influences, policy makers have become increasingly aware of the issue of informal care. The rather belated recognition of its central role in community care, together with the growing evidence of the burdens borne by some carers, has stimulated interest in assessing the impact and usefulness of services both in terms of relieving these strains and of supporting the continuance of informal care.

This discussion paper reviews work that has been done in the area of evaluating support to informal carers. It was prepared as part of the background to a larger study that has explored the relationship between carers and formal service support. The broad aim of that research has been to assist policy makers in developing more effective and appropriate forms of carer support.

Earlier work evaluating the impact of services tended to treat carers in a rather marginal fashion, mentioning their importance but relegating their activities and interests to the sideline. As interest in the subject of carers developed, it became clear that primary research was needed about the incidence, pattern and character of informal care if evaluation was to be able to encompass adequately this new carer aspect. Although the issue of the effectiveness of support to informal carers has never been absent from the research agenda, the broad trend of research has more recently concentrated elsewhere: exploring the situation of carers, the nature of caregiving and the burdens borne by carers. Research has therefore been more concerned with the social and psychological consequences and structuring of caregiving than with the impact of services them- selves. Parker provides a review of this literature up to 1985, extended in the second edition to 1990. (Parker, 1985, 1990).

Since the time of that review, work has progressed on, among other topics: the prevalence of caregiving (Green, 1988); the ethnography of caregiving (Cecil, Offer and St Leger, 1987); the normative expectations that underlie caregiving (Qureshi and Walker, 1989; Finch, 1989); the caregivers' own perceptions of caregiving (Hender- son, 1987); caregiving in the context of gender issues (Ungerson, 1987); the refinement of causes of stress in carers (Harpur and Lund, 1987); particular categories of carer, for example, single carers (Wright, 1986), or categories of relationship, for example, spouse carers (Parker, 1989) or carers who are daughters (Lewis and Meredith, 1988); black carers (Cameron et al, 1989); the financial consequences of caregiving (Glendinning, 1989); conceptual issues concerning the 'costing' of informal care (Wright, 1987).

It is not the purpose of this paper to review this developing literature. Rather, its scope is confined to research concerned with the evaluation of support to informal carers. The wider literature and the understandings that flow from it, however, form the background to this evaluative research, and at various points reference will be made to it.

Before moving on to the main subject of the book – work evaluating the effectiveness of services in support of carers – it is perhaps helpful to clarify some further points concerning the scope of the subject matter. The first of these relates to the concept of carer that is used, and the implications of this for evaluation. The second issue concerns the categorisation of carers, and the main client and patient groups that are covered in the review. The third issue concerns evaluation itself and the particular problems posed to evaluation by informal care. Lastly, we examine the scope of the services studied, raising the question of what counts as a service for carers. Each of these issues is discussed briefly in the following sections.

The concept of carer

The use of the term 'carer' has grown in the last decade. In its origins, it is an essentially professional service-oriented term. The word was itself developed within social care agencies and it bears the mark of that origin. The point is frequently made that many carers do not recognise themselves as such; the term is unfamiliar to them and, some would argue, at odds with how they perceive their actions, which they would regard as an extension of family or personal relations rather than in terms of being a carer, with its formal, quasi-employment overtones. Despite this, the currency of the term has grown. It is now widely used in government statements and has entered the political debate. Most important, it shows signs of translating relatively easily into the language of everyday life.

Conceptually, the term is a mixed one that lacks a clear analytic definition. It centres on the performance of tasks of a supportive character, but it also encapsulates elements of social and familial relationships. These are usually kin relations, although they extend to the bonds of friendship or neighbourliness where these have taken on the character of primary relationships. It is, however, often difficult to distinguish such carer relations from the ordinary patterns of care and dependency characteristic of family and gender relations; this is particularly the case with spouse carers. Associated with these relational features is the presence of affect: carer relations, if not defined in terms of emotion, are frequently associated with and energised by such, though clearly in more complex and ambiguous ways than the normative picture would suggest. Lastly – and perhaps most important – carer relations are frequently regarded, in both the carer's perception and that of the wider society, as involving some responsibility *for* the dependent person.

There is no simple definition of being a carer. An influential tradition in research has emphasised the performance of physical tasks, particularly where these go beyond the normal reciprocities between adults. Sometimes attempts are made to quantify these tasks in terms of the hours devoted to doing them. At least as onerous, however, can be the restriction imposed on carers by their need to oversee their dependants' well being on a day to day and, sometimes, moment to moment basis. Physical tasks performed for the person may not necessarily be the most important feature of the caregiving. Clearly there are differences here that relate to different forms of disability. Much of the carer literature has developed in the field of physical disability, particularly in relation to elderly people; the definitions need to be given a different emphasis when applied to the problems of caring for an adult with learning difficulties or with mental health problems. In these cases, the concept of 'being responsible for' the person achieves greater significance; though we would argue that such a concept is central to all definitions of being a carer.

Carer or informal sector?

In the light of the mixed character of the concept, some studies have preferred to employ the term 'informal sector'. This has the advantage of being formed analytically in relation to other social categories, and it is thus less ad hoc. It is also more inclusive in its scope, drawing in a range of potential supportive activities and relationships, and does not divorce caregiving from other forms of relationship. It also allows for important gradations of involvement, both over time and between individuals. It also avoids any over-emphasis on a single identified carer.

However, the focus of this paper remains around the concept of carer. This is partly because the trend of evidence concerning who cares for disabled people is clear: the burden of caregiving falls on certain close relationships. Different tasks are regarded as 'appropriate' to different relationships; there are structural limitations in the level of substitution one can expect between, for example, the tasks performed by friends and neighbours and those performed by close kin (Pancoast and Collins, 1976; Litwak and Kulis, 1983, Finch 1989). While not discounting the support given by neighbours and distant kin, such support tends to be circumscribed in character. Keeping an eye out for a neighbour or fixing a nail, though useful in themselves, do not constitute the real business of caregiving. Moreover, attempts to widen the conceptual scope to include the informal sector as a whole can lead to a systematic blurring of the real policy issues, whereby the realities of informal support to dependent people are lost in over-optimistic accounts of the community and its caring capacity (Allen, G., 1983). The heart of the problem of informal care concerns carers.

There is a second and equally important reason for concentrating on the concept of 'carer' rather than 'informal sector'. This is because it is in relation to the concept of carer that the real ambiguities and tensions of policy lie. In so far as agencies are primarily concerned with such carers as a form of resource – as part of the social world that provides the background to their work and the majority of care within society – a focus on the informal sector at large may be appropriate. But agencies cannot regard carers in quite the same way. They cannot adopt quite such separate and distant a view, for they themselves have obligations to carers that arise out of the particular character of the close caregiving relationship.

Social care agencies do not have serious ethical difficulties over their role in supporting people who are simply neighbours or other contacts in the social network because it is assumed that such distant relationships will evaporate should the burden become unacceptable. But where the individuals involved are bound by heavy obligations or close attachments, the actions of agencies are necessarily more complex and contain greater moral ambiguity. The element of obligation and the strains it may impose mean that carers are a legitimate object of concern for the welfare agencies. *Their* well-being or levels of stress need to be taken into account, and agencies cannot – openly at least – ignore the impact of their actions, or lack of actions, on this group. Carers cannot therefore be regarded simply as a kind of background resource – a social phenomenon whose nature agencies need to understand and which is best analysed as part of the informal sector in general; rather, they are a moral category towards which agencies themselves have obligations, however difficult they may find it to define these exactly.

It is important to understand this distinction between the concepts of carer and informal sector. This is not simply because it underwrites the use here of the concept of carer, but because it touches on what is the central dilemma in the evaluation of services in relation to carers. This is the ambiguous and uncertain position of carers within the social care system. Carers are rarely themselves the focus of an intervention. They are not clients or patients. They tend to exist 'off-centre' to what is the main concern with the client or patient. Yet their circumstances cannot be totally ignored by social care agencies, either because they are relevant to the continuance of caregiving and thus the capacity of the agency to fulfil its obligations, or because agencies themselves have obligations to relieve intolerable levels of strain.

The field of carer support is shot through with this tension between an instrumental interest in carers and a concern for their well-being *per se*. Though the issue has been explored more fully at a theoretical level by Twigg (1989), it has not by and large received adequate attention within the research literature reported here, nor in the accounts of practice developed by the service agencies themselves. As a result, thinking in this field is still very confused.

Established relations
In focusing on the carer, we have taken as our subject relationships that have already been so defined and labelled. Support for informal carers is interpreted here in terms of actions that support existing carers, rather than those that attempt to affect the overall availability or pattern of such care. This is partly to keep the scope of the subject within reasonable limits, but it reflects also a lack of evidence to suggest that such attempts to intervene at the macro-level of carer availability are in fact feasible. It is the nature of informal care that it is largely determined by the long-term structures of demography and kinship. These are in turn affected by current social and cultural patterns in regard to such factors as employment, the family and the expectations of women. Though affected by social policies to some degree, these factors determining the availability of informal care are largely beyond the scope of direct policy intervention.

We have therefore started our discussion from the point where the carer has already been defined as such. We are concerned with the factors that help carers to care, that improve their own well-being or quality of life, and that enable them to continue giving care. We do not discuss why they became carers, or whether more or different individuals might be encouraged to become such. Nor do we discuss issues around the social construction of dependency, and the potential for interventions that sustain independent living and thus short-circuit the need for informal care. All these are important issues. They are, however, beyond the scope of this book which is centrally concerned with *obligated relationships* and with individuals who are *already defined* as carers. They are the focus of the comments on services made below.

The categories of carers

There are three main ways in which carers are categorised: in terms of features of themselves (male carers, elderly carers), in terms of features of their dependant (carers of elderly people, carers of head injury patients), and in terms of their relationship (spouse carers, non-kin carers).

The majority of the recent studies of carers have restricted themselves to one or other of these categories. In relation to service evaluation, this has most commonly been in terms of features of the dependant, usually those relating to their client-group or patient status. There are obvious reasons for this in the patterns of service provision themselves, which tend to be organised along patient- or client-group lines. Such an approach, although it makes sense organisationally, does result in the problems faced by different groups of carers being studied in isolation. Work on the carers of elderly mentally infirm people has tended to progress separately from work on, for example, carers of adults with learning difficulties, though there are important parallels and contrasts to be drawn between the groups.

An alternative tradition has, by contrast, emphasised the undifferentiated character of caregiving. Many of the features and strains of caregiving – the restrictedness, the assumption of responsibility – are common across the dependency groups. Carers can experience similar problems regardless of whether the dependant is a physically disabled child, a mentally handicapped adult or a frail elderly person. There is a strong case to be made for regarding carers as a category in themselves, rather than subordinating them to the type of disability experienced by their dependant. The view that 'a carer is a carer is a carer' has been particularly important in the development of the carer lobby. The Association of Carers was one of the first groups to take such an inclusive approach, but the perception has also been influential in many of the new service developments which aim at a generic approach to carers.

In general, in this discussion paper we have adopted the generic approach. However, for reasons largely of space, certain limitations have been put on the range of carers that are included. The carers of mentally and physically disabled children have been excluded. This is essentially because the normative patterns of expectation that underlie the support of a child are different from those of an adult. Carers of mentally ill people, where that is the primary diagnosis, have also been excluded, again for reasons of the potentially different character and definition of the carer role in relation to this client group. Caring for someone with, for example, schizophrenia is often more episodic in character and focused around responsibility for the person, rather than direct care tasks. A companion publication by Perring, Twigg and Atkin (1990) *Families Caring for People Diagnosed as Mentally Ill: The Literature Re-examined* provides a review of this field.

This paper thus concentrates on the carers of elderly people and of younger mentally and physically disabled adults. In looking at the carers of elderly people, it includes those who care for dementia sufferers or for elderly people with some form of mental illness or difficulty where that is not the primary diagnosis.

As mentioned earlier, carers can be categorised in other ways. Some of these are demographic in character: male and female carers; elderly carers, child carers. Other categorisations relate to the relationship with the dependant: spouse carers, in-law carers; non-kin carers. Recent work has increasingly revealed the significance of these sub-categorisations. Care-giving is embedded in social relationships, and it is not surprising that these should fundamentally affect the meaning and impact of the tasks performed and the responsibilities undertaken. As a result, it is clear that future attempts to, for example, refine the causes of stress in carers, or examine the impact of different forms of help, need to incorporate these distinctions in their analysis. Carers should no longer be treated as quite so homogeneous a group as has been the practice so far.

Most of the literature that is reviewed here does not attempt to make such distinctions, at least in regard to the characteristics of carers: even fewer studies have attempted to tease out their implications for different forms of service support. Where distinctions are made in regard to the characteristics of carers, for example, as between the impact and relevance of a service for male and female carers, these will be noted.

Evaluation and its problems

In this review, we are concerned with evaluative research in relation to informal carers. We have here interpreted 'evaluation' in a broad sense, meaning any research that attempts to assess the impact, relevance or effectiveness of an intervention, whether the research is structured according to the classic evaluation methodology or not. Indeed, it has been one of the features of evaluation literature in the last decade that it has been concerned to break out of the straightjacket of the classic account of evaluation methodology and pursue more sophisticated and pluralist bases for its theory. These developments are welcome ones, particularly in the field of informal carers, where the relationship between inputs and outcomes, between clients and carers, between aims and methods, are particularly complex and ambiguous.

In surveying the literature, however, even where one takes a relatively inclusive definition of 'evaluation', one is struck by the relative lack of well-based studies. The field is not a highly developed one. There are a number of reasons for this.

There is the problematic context in which much of this research is undertaken. Many of the studies and reports referred to here have been produced in-house, often with limited resources and by practitioners and managers rather than professional researchers. Much of what has been produced is interesting and factually useful. It is rarely, however, particularly analytic or sophisticated in research terms and the significance of what is studied is largely unexamined. Evaluation, properly understood, requires all these qualities, and the lack of them severely limits the use that can be made of this work.

The reports that are published, moreover, can have a highly political character, often being produced to legitimise a service or justify a funding decision. It is striking how rare are the studies that conclude a service is ineffective or that a project should cease to be funded. It is difficult to know what kind of reliance can be placed on such material. The lack of studies of failed projects is a major flaw in this body of work, and much more could be learnt from franker accounts of the workings of schemes. Good process evaluation is just as absent in this field as is outcome evaluation. The internal politics of projects and the needs of individuals to pursue careers, however, make such developments unlikely.

Not all the work in the field is so closely embedded in the politics of service development. A number of better-based and more sophis- ticated pieces of work have been undertaken, and these are referred to in the following pages. It is true to say, however, that until relatively recently the lack of basic information about caregiving hampered the development of such work. We have already noted the relative novelty of informal care as a subject area, and it is only with the recent expansion of primary work that we can be said to know enough about the nature of caregiving to attempt to evaluate services in support of it. Even now, this knowledge is far from adequate.

An additional reason for the relative lack of evaluative work in this field relates more closely to the subject matter itself. The points made above concerning the political context of much research and the need for more basic understanding of the phenomena studied apply as much to the evaluation of services in general. There are, however, certain more intrinsic features of informal care that pose particular problems for the methodology of evaluation and mean that evaluation models, certainly of the classic type, are under considerable strain when applied to the subject of carers.

The central difficulty lies once again in the ambiguous position that carers occupy within the social care system. This poses a number of problems. The aims of policy, and thus of interventions, are vague and contradictory. How far should services be concerned with the well-being of carers as opposed to encouraging the continuance of caregiving? In certain situations, the two aims go together, but in many they do not. How should evaluation treat the close interrelationship of carer and dependant? Are all forms of support to the dependant to be regarded as forms of support to the carer, and what are the full implications of such an approach? How should conflicts of interest be treated?

Twigg has explored more fully elsewhere some of the theoretical difficulties posed to evaluation by the subject of informal care (Twigg, 1988). She has also outlined some of the problems posed to agencies in their conceptualisation of their relations with informal carers, and, in particular, in the tensions between regarding carers as resources, as co-workers and as co-clients (Twigg, 1989). By and large, evaluation work in this field has ignored these problems. They are rarely overtly acknowledged, though their disruptive influences are widely present in this literature. Little attention in general has been given to conceptual issues, and this has in turn weakened the quality of work in the field.

The scope of the services studied

One of the difficulties facing researchers in this field concerns what counts as a service for carers. It is helpful to regard this as having three distinct levels.

At the simplest level we have a range of services and schemes that have developed specifically to support carers, and that frequently have the words 'carers' or 'relative' in their title. Carer support groups provide a classic example of this, as do Crossroads Care Attendant Schemes. In addition, certain mainstream services – for example, respite services – are acknowledged to have an important carer function.

Turning to the second level, it is clear that carers also derive support from services that are not primarily aimed at them but at their dependant. This happens in two ways. It arises partly because service providers regard helping carers as an appropriate aspect of their work. This can either be because of a wish to maintain the support system of a dependant person, or because carers are regarded as needy in themselves. Either way, they may receive help from the services supporting dependent people, though, as we shall see, the degree to which these services allocate help to the carers of their clients or patients is limited. Despite this fact, there are good reasons to think that these forms of support provide the bulk of the formal help that carers do receive.

The process whereby carers are helped as a by-product of the provision of other services arises in a second way. Caring takes place within a relationship, which means there is a close interdependence between the cared for and the carer. As a result, there is a sense in which any help that is given to the dependant also helps the carer. Such interdependence does not preclude conflicts of interest between them, but it does mean that there is a certain artificiality in attempting to distinguish how far, for example, aids to independent living are provided to assist the carer or the dependant. This brings us to the third level.

Carers are part of 'the given', the taken-for-granted social world that provides the everyday background to service provision. It is against the realities of this taken-for-granted social world that support services of all types are structured. Services make assumptions about carers – their availability, their involvement, their duties – and, to a degree, structure their provision in the light of those assumptions. The issue of informal care thus permeates ordinary provision. As a result, any adequate attempt to review the relationship of formal services to informal care must go beyond simply those services that have a specific carer orientation, and look instead at the ways in which the social and health care systems as a whole are structured and operated in regard to carers. It must look at the network of embedded assumptions, rules and resource practices that structure the system generally in response to informal care.

The implications of such an understanding cannot be incorporated fully within the scope of this review. This is largely because so little work has been undertaken in terms of this perception. The bulk of what has been written concerning carers and services has not gone beyond the first stage – that of services specifically aimed at carers. A limited account of work has looked at the second stage – support for carers that comes as a by-product of other help. The third stage is almost entirely uncharted territory. We shall return to this issue when we look at ways in which future research might develop.

At a more conventional level, the services covered in this review include the three main sources of formal support to carers: social services, health services and the voluntary sector. There are other areas of public activity that are relevant to the support of carers, notably housing and the benefit system, but they are beyond the scope of this review. We note, however, their potential importance as part of the material and financial background to service provision. Glendinning (1989) has explored some of these financial and benefit issues.

Increasingly, there is a fourth sector; the private sector. There is some slight evidence of carers buying in forms of support, but the impact of such activity does not appear to be great (Maitland and Tutt 1987; Glendinning 1989). The subject deserves a passing mention partly because it is an element within the total pattern of services available and partly because of its implications for flexibility and choice. Changes within the social care system, some consequent on the 1989 White Paper on community care in the 1990s and others independently underway, may make the private, or quasi-private, sector more relevant. Such new patterns have as yet to emerge and clearly depend upon new financial structures.

A typology of support for carers

There is no exclusive typology of support for informal carers. Each has its merits and its limitations.

One very straightforward approach categorises services according to their source, dividing provision into the main service sectors – health, social services, voluntary and private. These sectors can in turn be sub-divided into their own organisational sectors: for example, acute hospital, community services and primary health care in the case of health; or residential and domiciliary in the case of social services. Such an approach follows much of the reality of community care. Services *are* organised along these dividing lines, and the different organisational sectors have a major impact on patterns of referral, assessment and practice. Many of the evaluation studies to which we shall refer are clearly rooted in these different service sectors.

Such an approach, however, ignores the degree to which certain forms of service are provided across the four sectors. Respite care is the classic example of this. It would be artificial and misleading to review the evaluation of respite in hospitals in isolation from, for example, that in residential homes or specialised voluntary sector units. Their themes are common ones.

The approach that will be taken in this review is a relatively conventional one. It places the carer at the heart of the subject matter, and groups services in relation to the different types of contribution they make to the situation of the carer. The carer rather than the dependant becomes the main focus.

As with all such typologies, however, it has certain limitations, and these need to be mentioned briefly. As will be clear, the approach assumes a certain relationship of responsibility. Services *assist* the carer to do certain tasks, or *relieve* the carer from doing them. Implicit in this is an assumption that the carer is already defined as such and that the responsibility for the dependant lies with them. The danger of such an approach is that while it recognises the importance of the carer and places him or her at the centre of things, it can at the same time lock the carer more firmly into a relationship of responsibility that many have been concerned to question (Finch, 1984; Dalley, 1988). The usefulness of the typology should not, therefore, lead us to ignore alternative conceptions of responsibility, nor to fail to address issues of the proper balance of responsibility between formal and informal sources of care (Finch, 1987; Glendinning, 1987; Jordan, 1987). Services should not simply be seen as a means of shoring up carers. Such issues are beyond the scope of this review, but their implications will be touched on at various points; for example, in relation to the possible role of services in allowing caregiving to cease.

The typology is also one that, in assuming the responsibility of the carer, does not attempt to address the ways in which dependency itself is socially structured. As we have already noted, people can be forced to depend upon their carers because the ways in which the physical and social environment is structured impede their aspirations for independent living. This is a theme of particular significance for younger disabled people, but it applies to all dependent groups.

According to the typology suggested, services in relation to carers fall into five broad categories:

First there are the services aimed at the *carer per se*. Carer support groups provide the clearest example of this. Their central aim is *to relieve the pressures of caregiving and help the carer to manage more adequately the emotional strains that arise from it*. There are aspects of a number of services that also relate to this aim, whether directly through social work counselling or indirectly through the supportive role of professionals, such as doctors and nurses, or of grades of staff, such as home helps whose job descriptions may not officially extend to emotional encouragement and support but who clearly provide it.

The second set of services are those concerned with *assisting the carer with practical tasks*. The activities here can be various, but often centre around the performance of domestic or personal care tasks. Relevant services include home helps, home carers, care assistants and nursing auxiliaries. Services that substitute collective and external forms of provision for individual and domestic ones are also relevant: for example, incontinence laundries or meals on wheels. Aids and adaptations can be relevant here.

The third set are services that assist the carer by *providing relief from caring*. This can be achieved in a number of ways: by forms of day care, sitting services, respite and phased care, fostering and holiday provision.

Fourthly, there are interventions designed to *enable the carer to get more from the care system and from his or her own abilities*. These cover various forms of advice service, whether welfare rights or informational outreach.

Lastly, there are the *level and quality of services provided to the dependant*. As we have seen, determining what is a service for carers as opposed to dependants is very difficult. High quality, well-resourced professional help can maximise the well-being and independence of the dependant and in doing so, also relieve the anxieties and burdens of the carer. These services include, as well as acute treatment, all forms of rehabilitation that encourage the dependant to have a more independent life.

Looking at the field in this way soon reveals how patchy the research evidence is. Research tends to be based around services rather than around the performance of particular types of task or the meeting of particular needs. As a result, many forms of support have been neglected; never made subject to conscious scrutiny, let alone evaluation. Evaluations typically focus on small-scale innovative services. They are much less often concerned with specific aspects of mainstream services. Even less are they concerned with the impact and effectiveness of such services as GP support or acute medical care. The impact of medicine on carers is a particularly poorly researched area, but this lack of information applies also to other forms of 'service' such as social work where recognition, assessment and gate-keeping are as significant as actual service provision. As a result, many of the 'boxes' in the typology are relatively empty, and there is little evaluative work to report in relation to them.

The review that follows is broadly structured according to the typology. At times it will adopt a more service-orientated and substantive approach in which the main services will be discussed in turn. This is largely because that is how the majority of the literature has been structured. Each section will start with a discussion of the role of the service in support of carers, and will then move on to review the evaluative research that has been undertaken in relation to the particular service.

PART TWO

Services in support of carers

Carer support groups and information services

It may seem unusual to start a review of services in support of carers with the carer support groups, as these are not commonly regarded as central to needs of carers. However, of all forms of service, they offer the one that is most directly focused on the carer him or herself. The primary aim of such groups is the support of carers, and the definition of their remit is cast in terms of the carer rather than the dependant. This is in marked contrast to the majority of provision where carers are, at best, secondary clients.

The forms of activity and organisation that are encompassed by the term 'carer support group' are diverse. There is a variety of dimensions on which one might attempt to classify them. One can take, for example, the organisational basis. Is the group profession-ally organised by therapists or social workers, or is it self-help? This is a critical distinction. If it is self-help, is it part of a national charity which promotes and supports such activities, or is it a small local group, gathered informally? What are the sources of its funding? Some groups rely solely on the fundraising capacity of members, whereas others are externally funded, supported by the statutory agencies. Some groups are generic in their approach, attracting all types of carers; others are focused around specific client groups. If the latter, do the consequences of the differences between the forms of dependency affect the character of the group? Whether the group is closed or open in its membership, whether it is time-limited or continuing, how large the membership is: all affect its nature. Whether it is an off-shoot of another form of service can also define its character, and this can have implications for the ways in which its effectiveness is judged.

Groups also differ in their aims and functions: these can be primarily social and recreational, providing a venue for talking and relaxing, an escape from the situation at home; or they can be much more strongly emotional and expressive, allowing for the release of feeling and the sharing of experience. They can be oriented to information and training. They can provide channels of contact between carers and professionals. They can be focused around pressure-group action at the local or national level. In practice, carer support groups typically involve a mixture of these elements, though as we shall see, there are some systematic differences in emphasis.

The broad classification adopted here is based on a mixture of organisational control and primary focus of activity. This suggests six main forms which will be discussed in greater detail:

- the *self-help group* run by and for carers

- a sub-variant of this, the *voluntary centre* where carers meet and support each other informally

- the carer group that is an off-shoot of a *service facility*, for example, a day hospital

- differing from this in intent but sharing the professional control, *groups set up to train or educate carers*

- the *therapy group* model, rare in Britain but included here for its relevance to other forms

- groups set up by, for example, social workers that form an *intermediate category* between those that are service dominated and those that are fully self-help in character.

Before discussing the implications of these differing forms, we should perhaps make a general comment about the literature in this area. This concerns the absence of good ethnographic accounts of how carer groups actually operate. There are descriptions of sessions to be found in such service provider journals as *Community Care* and *Social Work Today*, but these accounts tend to be rather uncritical and dominated by the perceptions of professionals as to what happens at such events and what constitutes legitimate activity. Though the literature sometimes lists the various activities of the groups such as mutual support, lobbying, socialising, etc, these are rarely explored or analysed in any depth. As a result, what evaluative research there is tends to be over-dominated by the tradition that derives from the analysis of therapy groups. As we shall see, this model is not entirely inappropriate. It has certainly been very influential in the minds of many professionals who run carer groups. It does however impose a rather limited range on the analysis that does not always reflect the complexity of what is being studied. Such an approach also tends to make assumptions that a common, quasi-therapeutic, interpretation of the group and its aims is shared between the attenders and the professionals, whether they be practitioners or researchers. A fuller ethnography of the groups might show this to be mistaken.

The self-help groups

A considerable literature has developed in recent years concerned with self-help groups. Much of this has been American, and most has been concerned with people suffering directly from a disability rather than with their carers. Richardson and Goodman (1983), however, did include carer-orientated groups organised by the National Council for Carers and their Elderly Dependants, in their wider study of self-help. Pancoast, Parker and Froland (1983), Hinrichsen, Revenson and Shinn (1985) and Llewelyn and Haslett (1986) provide reviews of the area.

Groups exist for a variety of personal, social and medical problems. Although they vary considerably in their structure and purpose, they share certain fundamental characteristics. Hinrichsen et al (1985) have outlined these as follows. First, they are composed of individuals who share a common problem and a common desire to provide support to others in the same circumstances. Second, members meet on a regular basis to share personal experiences, discuss coping solutions, provide mutual support, and identify community resources. Third, the groups are sanctioned, structured and controlled by group members so that the provision of help relies primarily on members' skills, knowledge and concern.

In the field of carers, such groups take a variety of forms. Although national bodies like the Carers' National Association or the Alzheimer's Disease Society do offer guidelines and support in the establishment of local groups, their exact format and character is dependent on the interests, enthusiasms and abilities of the local members. *Caring Together*, produced by the King's Fund Informal Caring Support Unit together with the National Extension College, is an example of material providing advice and guidelines for the establishment of carer self-help and support groups (Wilson, 1988). Forster (1985) also gives advice on running a support group for carers of dementia sufferers.

Characteristically, such groups offer a mixture of social and emotional support within the group, together with information sessions. Groups can also be active in local lobbying of service providers. In addition, the groups have a role in supporting the national activities of their associations. Such lobbying and advocacy form an important function of the groups, though they are not the primary focus of this review.

Some groups, such as the Carers' National Association (formally the Association of Carers and the National Council for Carers and their Elderly Dependants), are generic in their membership; while others focus on particular dependency groups, for example, the carers of stroke victims, of people with dementia or head injuries, of mentally handicapped adults, or of people suffering from particular diseases such as Parkinson's Disease. In all of these cases, there are relevant associations running groups in support of carers.

With self-help groups the sessions are not professionally led, though certain individuals inevitably tend to take on key roles in their development and activity (Richardson, 1983). The absence of professional involvement is a defining feature of such groups; and many of the voluntary bodies, particularly the Carers' National Association, emphasise the importance of this independence from service providers and professionals. Though not set up, as some self-help groups have been, in direct conflict with professionals (Llewelyn and Haslett, 1986), these carer associations do maintain an independent and somewhat critical stance. This is particularly for their lobbying role, but it carries over also into their attitude to group sessions which appear to be regarded much more as the property of the carers themselves than is the case with the sessions dominated by professionals.

The absence of professionally trained group leaders can, however, impose constraints. The expression of very powerful feelings can in such contexts prove threatening, more than the group on its own is able to manage. This is an issue of which the Alzheimer's Disease Society, among other groups, has been aware. Such powerful feelings are, of course, characteristic of the situation of some carers, and the cathartic effects that have been identified as a central feature of support groups may therefore be muted where the form of the group is not structured to deal with such expression. This point should not be over-emphasised, however. The impression gained from accounts of carer groups in the UK is that such confiding and supporting occurs mainly informally and between individuals, rather than in the open sessions. The informal, and often purely social aspects of the meeting, can be the most valuable.

Throughout the literature on carer support groups, one theme of central importance emerges and this is the element of mutual support. Thus Glosser and Wexler (1985) in an evaluation of a series of support groups for the carers of sufferers of dementia found:

> The highest positive evaluations [by participants] were given to factors such as 'finding out how others are dealing with their

problems', 'getting a chance to meet other people with similar problems', 'sharing feeling with others', and 'getting support from other group members'. (p. 233)

This very clear message is borne out more generally in the self-help literature, where Hinrichsen et al. conclude that self-help groups' 'central strength derives from *mutual peer* support'. They emphasise how a review of numerous studies underscores how 'from the members' perspective, it is the opportunity to meet others with similar problems that is the most beneficial aspect of group participation' (Hinrichsen et al., 1985, p.66-7).

Beyond this, the self-help literature suggests that the balance between the various elements in the group's functions will vary quite considerably with the sorts of problems faced by the participants. No single format is best. Llewelyn and Haslett's study (1986) demonstrates how the perceived helpfulness of self-help groups relates to differing concerns of members. A group concerned with social and personal support for widows found the experience of knowing you are not alone in your problems the most helpful, and the opportunity for self-disclosure the least. A group formed around actual physical illness, however, favoured information and guidance, while again not favouring self-disclosure. A group for depressives emphasised the benefits of the social cohesion the group offered and found direct guidance of little help.

It is likely that similar patterns of helpfulness relate to the situations of carers. As yet, no detailed study has been undertaken on these lines, and exact data on the types of group activity that are favoured by carers is not available. Anecdotal evidence suggests, unsurprisingly, that individual carers vary both in the degree to which they find such groups appealing and in the mix of activities and functions that they find helpful. Little or no attention has been paid to such systematic differences.

Carer support centres
Not all the mutual self-help support that carers receive takes place within formally constituted groups. Some carer associations have preferred to establish a physical centre to be a focus for services, information and social support. Such centres can be seen as operating in parallel ways to those of the carer groups, though without the level of emotional charge and self-disclosure that closed membership and defined boundaries can allow.

The model of the centre is perhaps more characteristic of associations formed around a particular dependency group than of those catering for the generic category of carers. The Alzheimer's Disease Society together with Cleveland Social Services has established a flexible respite care facility that has in addition a drop-in centre where carers can come for information and social support (Farries, 1985). The Wallasey Carers' Care Centre provides a more unusual mix, combining an incontinence launderette with a place for carers to meet and exchange information (Melville, 1987). The evaluation of such mixed activities is difficult, and there is, as a result, little other than descriptive literature to draw on.

Groups that are off-shoots of a facility

Perhaps in greatest contrast to the voluntary self-help carer groups are those established by professionals as off-shoots of another service. These services are typically medical in orientation. Smith and Cantley (1985) analyse a relative support group attached to a psychogeriatric day hospital; Mykyta, Bowling, Nelson and Lloyd (1976) describe a relative support group established as part of the work of a rehabilitation unit for stroke patients; and Fuller et al. (1979), North (1985) and Hettiaratchy and Manthorpe (forthcoming) discuss groups for the carers of patients of hospital-based psychiatric services.

The essential features and rationale of such groups are very similar to those of the self-help groups. The expression of feelings, the mutual support, and the gains to be made from shared experience are all emphasised in both the overt aims and actual practice of such groups. These groups, however, have certain additional features which are characteristic of their origins. We shall therefore assume the shared background and concentrate here only on these particular features.

The first concerns the relationship to the facility. Such groups often play a particular role in bringing relatives into contact with the service, expanding their levels of information and trust, and bringing them into the orbit of the service. Hettiaratchy and Manthorpe (forthcoming) in particular bring out the ways in which carer groups can act as a bridge for the carer, increasing his or her knowledge of the world of the hospital and confidence in making contact with it. One carer commented:

> It's a rather strange divided life we lead. One part at home trying to be normal, the other part wondering what's going on here. (Hettiaratchy and Manthorpe, forthcoming.)

At times, the groups' functions become rather like that of the Parent Teacher Association. Some also operate as a focus for local fund raising, acting as the Friends of the unit or facility. This is particularly characteristic of the parents' groups that are attached to adult training centres.

The second particular feature is the degree to which these groups are professionally dominated. It is not simply that they have facilitators who are professionals, but that a number of professionals involved in the facility are commonly in attendance; in Smith and Cantley's account, a ratio of five professionals to ten carers. This clearly affects the dynamics and power relations within the group. Professionals also control the resources of the group. Mykyta et al. (1976) describe how, in their group for the supporters of stroke victims, carers were asked to terminate their membership once the waiting list started to build up. This decision was in the control of the professionals, and the group represented a resource for them to allocate. Such an approach is very different from that of a group constituted and controlled by the carers themselves.

Smith and Cantley provide the most sophisticated account of some of the tensions that relate to these features, and we shall follow their analysis quite closely. They identified five distinct functions of the carer support group they studied, which was established as part of the service offered by a psychogeriatric day hospital.

The first function related to the exchange of information. Patients were normally the only channel of communication between the day hospital and the home, but this posed obvious problems. The group allowed a two-way exchange of information. In addition, it allowed staff to present to relatives an image of the hospital as an active therapeutic institution.

The second function was to allow for individual consultation. Demands for individual consultation by relatives within the day hospital were experienced by staff, particularly medical staff, as disruptive in that they demanded time and possibly resources. Channelling them into a group forum helped to contain their impact, while maintaining the ideology that the institution was open to relatives.

The third function concerned providing explanations of resource allocations. Staff reported with approval how the group operated to control the harassment of consultants by relatives pressing for the institutionalisation of their dependant.

What Smith and Cantley term 'negotiating the condition' provided the fourth function, with staff emphasising a therapeutically optimistic view in contrast to the more pessimistic beliefs of the carers.

Lastly, the group provided therapy for the carers. Smith and Cantley emphasise that the group did provide a venue for the expression of pent-up feelings. Carers did gain relief, particularly from the shared storytelling and the often macabre humour that this can provide. But it did so, they argue, in ways that limited the level of expression, and that kept expression away from channels that might challenge the hospital.

Smith and Cantley's account is very different from that provided in the majority of the literature where the benefits to relatives are emphasised, but where little attention is paid to the ways such groups benefit the staff or institutions that run such groups. They provide a timely reminder both of the complexity of what is being studied and of the need to be aware of the multiple layers of interest that often lie behind rather bland evaluations of the effectiveness of services.

Training courses for carers

The promotion of basic information is part of the activity of most carer support groups. It is a common feature in both the self-help and professionally-led group sessions to have invited speakers to discuss practical matters.

Some forms of carer support, however, concentrate exclusively on such practical aspects. Training courses for carers commonly focus on basic nursing skills such as lifting, the prevention of pressure sores and the management of incontinence. Saddington (1984), McLachlan, Sheard and Anderson (1985) and Billington (1987) describe such courses.

The accounts provided by Saddington and by McLachlan et al., however, point to some of the limitations of such an approach. Saddington's course was originally intended to focus very much on nursing skills but: 'it became apparent after the first evening that the needs of these carers were much more complex than we thought . . . Many carers desperately needed someone to talk to . . . [and] the course programme was rearranged'.

The course organised by McLachlan et al. was an off-shoot from the hospital service and underwent a similar development. Response to the initial, strongly instructional, format was discouraging: by the fifth and sixth sessions, attendance had dwindled to nothing. As a result, the evenings were restructured to provide a more clearly supportive as well as informational format; in this form they proved popular, with an average attendance of 28.

These examples illustrate the problems that arise from seeing caring too narrowly in terms of task performance. It is not that such practical training and advice for carers is of no worth, but that it does not meet the full range of their needs and, furthermore, does not alone provide a particularly useful focus for meetings. From the point of view of service providers, such courses have an attraction and a rationale. They are relatively easy to organise and they fit within the traditions of a professional approach. As such, they demonstrate the way thinking about carer support is still dominated by the perceptions of professionals rather than actual experiences of carers.

The trend of the literature suggests that the nursing and paramedical services should target their resources as educators more on existing carer groups that have a more established, organic basis rather than attempting to establish discrete training courses.

The therapy group or counselling model
The therapy group model properly speaking is not one that occurs with any frequency in relation to carer support. Most accounts of professionally-led groups disclaim any such description; many in the carer associations find such therapeutic orientations patronising.

A reference has been included to this approach, however, because it is a model that exerts considerable influence on all group work, and because it points up, yet again, some of the issues in relation to support groups established and controlled by service providers.

In general, the literature describing carer support groups that have a stronger counselling or therapy orientation derives from North America. This is largely a reflection of the greater receptiveness of American culture to psychotherapeutic practice, but it reflects also the fact that the professionals offering group therapy or support are less likely to be associated directly with service provision. The impression from this American carer literature is one of a much clearer emphasis on the carer, on personal growth, maturity and making good decisions (Hausman, 1979; Hartford and Parsons, 1982). Among these good decisions can be the decision to cease giving care.

Hausman, evaluating a series of time-limited counselling groups for carers of elderly parents, described their three main goals as: that of finding a balance between responsibility to one's self, one's nuclear family, and one's parents; that of setting limits on the extent of the members' duties and obligations to their parents; and that of learning to deal with one's parents in a mature way, leaving aside the conflicts, rebellions and unresolved issues from childhood that interfere with objective evaluations of real needs. (Hausman, 1979, p.103)

None of these aims is alien to carer support groups as they operate in Britain. However, the impression from this American literature is one of a much greater emphasis on carers as people with their own choices and their own concerns, rather than more simply on their role as the carers of someone. This clearer focus on the carer may be the product of the fact that the professionals organising such groups are less inclined to see them as an extension of other work with the dependant or as a means of containing or managing a publicly acknowledged responsibility for the frail and dependent. They do thus appear to be more free of the element of manipulation that can lie behind groups organised within the service sector.

Social work enabled groups
We come finally to what is an intermediate form, lying between the self-help and the more professionally dominated models. These are the carer support groups established, and sometimes led, by a social worker, but operating in the locality and not attached to any particular service.

There has been no systematic review of the range and number of such groups. However, it is probably fair to assume that such groups have now been established, at least for a time, in the majority of local authorities. There is some evidence for their establishment as a response to the pressures of bombardment, though they appear more commonly to arise out of ordinary practice, whereby workers become aware of the situation of carers locally and want to respond (Rice, 1984; Brunswick, 1986). A carer support group offers a potentially low-cost solution to these problems. Such groups are also often established as part of the work of a development officer or specialist worker, particularly for the elderly. They are probably the commonest form of response to the issue of carer support. The aim is usually to set up and encourage the group in its early stages, but gradually to wean it away from professional support, towards the autonomous self-help model.

Once again, systematic evaluation of such projects is lacking. Anecdotal evidence suggests that a number of schemes, contrary to expectations, experience difficulties in recruiting members. This may be a result of the well-known problems of contacting carers, and of getting carers to perceive themselves in that role. There can also be practical barriers to attendance if the group cannot provide substitute care for the dependant while the carer is out. This is a problem that is shared across the different forms of group. The difficulties in recruitment may, however, be evidence of the limited attraction of such groups to the majority of carers. Many carers have limited free time and limited opportunities to get out. They may wish to spend what opportunities they do have in getting away from their situation, rather than talking about it. Anecdotal informal evidence also suggests that the transition from agency-enabled to self-help status can be difficult and that many groups founder once the particular post-holder has moved on.

Information services

One of the important functions performed by carer groups is the transmission of information. This often occurs informally between individual carers who benefit from the knowledge and experience of others in the same situation. This appears, anecdotally at least, to be a major source of information both about the nature and course of the problems from which dependants suffer and about the services that others have obtained locally to help them. This latter form of information can be particularly important in view of the oblique and discretionary character of much provision for informal carers. Many carers learn of important forms of support only by hearing of what others have received.

A number of local authorities have attempted to provide information to carers in more systematic ways, producing carer handbooks that outline a range of local services and support groups. The *Handbook for Carers* produced by North Yorkshire Social Services Department (nd, 1986, 1987) provides a well-produced example. Such A-Zs of services for carers have proved increasingly popular with local authorities. The Birmingham Special Action Project has published a range of high-quality literature aimed at informal carers, advising them of forms of support. It has also produced literature on the (future) rights of carers under the Disabled Persons Act.

Resource centres have similarly taken on an information function. Some such centres, as we have noted, are specifically designed for carers; others provide information to carers as part of a general support strategy for particular client groups. The proposed resource centre for mental handicap services in South Tyneside is an example of the latter.

The Kings Fund Informal Care Unit has, in particular, developed this information side, commissioning a number of publications to assist carers. These include *Taking a Break* (Kings Fund, 1987) and *Caring at Home* (Kohner, 1988), as well as a quarterly magazine, *Carelink*. The unit has also produced two brief publications designed to help local groups prepare and disseminate information about sources of help. *Guidelines for Compiling Local Information on Taking a Break* (Kings Fund, 1987) outlines suggested material to be covered in relation to respite. *Making a Splash* (Kings Fund, 1989) concentrates on strategies for local dissemination. The Kings Fund Unit has also been active in developing training videos and assisting in the production of television programmes designed to educate and inform the public. The voluntary sector has also been active in this field, producing both local guides and national literature. A good example of the latter is the booklet produced by the Alzheimer's Disease Society, *Caring for the Person with Dementia: A Guide for Families and Other Carers* (1984).

The rather diffuse character of these information activities and – particularly at the local authority level – the relatively low budget that attaches to them, means that there is no directly evaluative material for us to review.

There are, however, some obvious criticism that can be made. Information alone does not ensure the availability of support, and many carers have complained that lists of services or voluntary-sector phone numbers are of little use if the facilities are over-subscribed and the support effectively unavailable. Information booklets, in the absence of any service development, can appear to be little more than low cost, token responses. In addition, so much support for carers is discretionary; only available on the say so of professionals. This is particularly true of medical sources of help. Carers need therefore not only to be told of the existence of various forms of support, but also of how they can successfully go about obtaining that support. Accessing professional systems is not always easy. Lastly, information, though it puts power in the hands of carers does so only if they themselves think it appropriate for them to use it. As important for many carers as information, is the permission to use it.

Help with domestic and personal care tasks

Practical assistance with domestic and personal care tasks provides the second major form of help. Here the exercise of disentangling services provided for the carer from those provided for the dependant becomes more difficult. In a sense, they cannot be separated, since all activity in this area that assists the dependant has some impact on the situation of the carer.

A certain degree of separation is, however, made by service providers. Some services are specifically provided only where carers are 'unavailable'. The most notable example of this is – as we shall see – the home help service. But the practice of effectively rationing support services in terms of the availability or otherwise of informal care is relatively widespread within the service network. It certainly applies within the community nursing service, particularly in relation to bathing, but it appears also to be an implicit assumption behind the allocation of many forms of support, from day care to transport.

The assumption of the 'availability' of informal care often appears to be interpreted here in terms of household structure, though this is not the only criterion. It tends to be assumed that where the dependent person shares a household with someone else, that person will provide practical support. As a result, there is a striking contrast, with regard to service receipt, between carers who share a household with their dependant and those who do not. Household structure clearly plays a central role in defining whether carers are regarded as individuals holding prime responsibility for the care of the dependant, or as individuals who assist, together with other agencies, in the care of the dependant. This corresponds in some degree to the distinction between carers as resources and carers as co-workers (Twigg, 1989).

The home help service

It is a feature of the home help service that it is targeted predominantly on those living alone, and this pattern of allocation appears to be growing (Cooper, 1986; Social Service Inspectorate, 1987b). This emphasis on those living alone has obvious implications for carers. There has been a tradition in some local authorities, particularly in the past, of specifically excluding from eligibility for home help any elderly people who live with younger household members. In some authorities, this has been an explicit policy rule, but it exists more commonly elsewhere at the level of practice. Some authorities – for example, Tameside – have explicitly altered their policies to include the support of carers as a legitimate aim for the service, but such moves are slow and likely to be hampered by the traditional bias of the service towards the unsupported.

As a result of this bias in provision towards clients who live alone, the home help service is not usually conceived of as of central importance to the support of carers. Levin, Sinclair and Gorbach, however, in an article on the role of the home help service in supporting carers of elderly mentally infirm people argue forcibly for its potential significance (Levin et al., 1985), and we shall draw on their article at some length. The claim they make is important: first, because it is based on a large-scale evaluative study (reported in greater detail in Levin et al, 1983); second, because it takes the carer rather than the dependant as the focus; third, and most significantly, because it addresses the impact of a mainstream service. By and large, what evaluation there has been concerning the impact of services on carers has related to innovative, specialist schemes, with all the problems that arise from such a focus on the small-scale and pioneering. But as Levin, Sinclair and Gorbach argue, most carers '. . . have to rely on the mainstream health and social services. Expenditure on these services is far greater than on innovations.' (p.1) The home help service is of particular significance since it is, in terms of both levels of expenditure and of levels of contact, the single most important local authority service supporting elderly people.

Levin et al. draw attention to the possible consequences for carers of the pattern of allocation of the service:

> Confused old people who lived alone and were supported by relatives nearby were nearly twice as likely as those living in the same household as their supporting relatives to have been provided with home help. (p.3)

As a result, 'the elderly persons most likely to have home helps were those whose supporters, in the light of several measures, carried the least heavy loads.' (p.3)

This pattern of burden was overwhelmingly the result of the strains faced by people who shared their home with an elderly confused person. It applied to a range of problems:

> supporters who gave most practical help with personal care were far less likely than others to have home helps. So too were those who coped with severe dementia, those who coped with faecal incontinence, those who coped with many 'problem behaviours', those who faced a high number of key problems and those who showed signs of severe strain. (Levin et al, p.3)

From the viewpoint of the carers, there was an inverse relationship between the severity of the problems faced and the likelihood of receiving support from the home help service. This bias appears from the General Household Survey figures to be a more general feature of service provision (Green, 1988).

The article by Levin et al. goes on to argue, however, that the home help service could be highly relevant to the difficulties faced by these carers. First, they demonstrate how the service can address some, though not all, of the problems faced by these supporters. They mention, in particular, direct relief over household tasks, providing a break and a chance to have 'an opportunity for everyday exchanges' for those cut off from ordinary conversation with their dependant. Second, they demonstrate the desire for the service by, a proportion at least, of supporters. (The exact significance of the different proportions is hard to interpret from their account.)

Third, and most significantly, they demonstrate the relevance of the service in terms of its direct impact on the well-being of the supporters. They do this by comparing scores on the General Health Questionnaire (GHQ) at two periods in time. During this period, the dependants of some carers either died or went into institutions. Evidence of the stressful impact of caring and the relief afforded by no longer having to do so is provided by the improvement in the GHQ scores of those carers whose dependants had entered institutions or died, compared with those whose dependants did not. However, comparing the scores of carers who did and did not receive home help suggests that the service is able at least to cushion the deleterious effects of caregiving. Thus:

> Among those still looking after their relatives the increase in strain, as measured by mean differences in GHQ score, was on average less if the supporters had home helps than if they did not. Among those whose relatives were living in institutions the reduction in the level of strain was greater in those without home helps . . . Overall, therefore, the home help service seemed to reduce the benefit to psychological health which supporters would gain from admission of their relatives to an institution. (p.5)

More elaborate analysis that adjusted the estimated advantage of the initial GHQ and various relevant characteristics of the supporter and the old person reduced the statistical relationship but did not remove it.

The evidence of the Levin study is particularly significant because it suggests that services do not always need to address directly the focus of the problem. For some of the recipients, the focus of the problem may indeed have been housework-type tasks, but a range of research in relation to the carers of elderly mentally infirm people has suggested that stress arises less from the performance of physical tasks than from what Gilleard, following Hirschfield, terms the 'loss of mutuality' and the destruction of the relationship between the carer and the dependant (Gilleard, 1984). To influence this directly through the provision of services is almost impossible. It is extremely hard even to influence the actions and behaviour that signal this deterioration. Evidence that suggests that services which have an impact elsewhere in the supporters' lives can help their overall levels of stress is particularly significant for the support of an otherwise difficult to help and highly stressed group.

Beyond this evidence of a generally favourable outcome in relation to home help services, the Levin study found certain differences in the level of impact between sub-groups of carers. This pattern emerged as a result of examining a different outcome measure. This was the likelihood of admission of the dependant to an institution. Here the study found that the impact of home help was experienced differentially between male and female carers. Thus, 'old people supported by men were quite likely to enter institutions if they did not have the home help service but much less likely to do so, if they did.' However, 'if the supporters were women, their elderly relatives were very unlikely to enter institutions irrespective of the home help service.'

Levin et al. suggest that this differential impact may be a result of the 'different personal meaning' of receipt of the service to women for whom the performance of household tasks, unlike for men, was part of their normal expectation and self identity. Ramdas (1986) in her study of women carers makes a similar point. She found that the traditional gender assumptions held by her respondents led them to regard domestic tasks as a 'private' matter, and therefore home help, and to some degree meals on wheels, as inappropriate forms of support for them. She goes on to comment:

> However desirable it may be to attack the gender divisions of labour in caring, the data from the interviews suggests that it is useless to provide services which interfere with normal domestic routines, as these services will not be accepted by the carers. (Ramdas, 1986, p.108)

To discover whether the situation is indeed as Ramdas suggests in her rather strongly expressed conclusion requires further research. However, she does point out one of the difficulties involved in setting up services that are responsive to people's preferences or, at least, preferences as they are initially expressed. Part of the difficulty in this area relates to gaining an adequate assessment of the potential acceptability and impact of the service from potential recipients that does not simply reflect superficial social and cultural judgements. This is a recurring theme when discussing the assessment of the acceptability of services, particularly services that have not pre-viously been experienced.

The issue also raises questions of equity between men and women. Arber et al. in their analysis of the 1980 General Household Survey demonstrate some evidence of gender discrimination in relation to the provision of home help to married women (Arber et al., 1988). The picture is complex because of the interaction between gender and household and marital status. Unlike earlier work, based mainly on small samples, Arber et al. found no significant difference in the level of provision to single female as opposed to single male carers. They did find, however, that the provision of domiciliary services discriminated against *married* female carers who were assumed to be available to give support even though they might also be in work.

How far such patterns are the result of the assumptions and values of service providers, and how far they reflect the wishes, or at least the initially expressed wishes, of carers and clients, is unclear. Authorities, however, do need actively to consider issues of equity. Simply re-targeting the home help service on carers, where gender assumptions are operating perhaps on both sides, could result in a more, rather than less, gender-biased pattern of service.

Care attendant schemes

Related to the home help service, but with a rather different emphasis, is a variety of care attendant schemes that provide an intensive and flexible form of domiciliary care. The functions they perform are various and not confined to domestic and personal care assistance, though that is at the centre of their activity. In addition, they provide general emotional and social support to both the dependant and the carer, as well as offering the carer an opportunity for a break from the dependant. They overlap to a considerable degree with various services providing respite care to the supporter which will be discussed further below.

The best known of such schemes are those of the Crossroads Care Attendants, first set up in 1974 (Bristow, 1981). Some 127 schemes are in operation, helping 9,000 disabled and elderly people and their carers (Crossroads, 1987). They are organised within the voluntary sector and form a group of schemes which are held together in loose federation. Though they all have the same objective, they vary in their format and organisation. Other parallel forms of care attendant scheme have developed both within the voluntary and statutory sectors. A 1984 survey of London boroughs, for example, identified 17 such schemes, of which only seven were Crossroads affiliated (Hopper and Roberts, nd).

The schemes vary in the degree to which they emphasise their role in carer support. In the Crossroads schemes, this is the central aim.

Cooper, in his evaluation of Crossroads schemes in Essex, praises this emphasis and contrasts it with other community services where 'beneficial impacts on carers' situations have tended to be a matter of happy coincidence' (Cooper, 1986, p.24).

Some of the other care attendant schemes do take on disabled people where no carer is involved and where the support is offered simply for the dependent person. Lovelock's study of three schemes in Hampshire found that in 12 per cent of cases there was no carer involved. However, in the remaining majority of cases, various forms of carer support were seen as part of the central activity of the work. In 16 per cent of cases, it was impossible to determine whether the service was to assist the disabled person or the highly distressed carer. In a further six per cent the carer was scarcely able to continue, and the attendant was provided to prevent complete care breakdown. In 12 per cent of cases, the main involvement was to sustain and relieve the carer and to allow him or her to get out of the house. In 13 per cent of cases, the attendant allowed the carer to work; and in a further 9.5 per cent, the attendant was provided to allow the carer to support other dependants or children. Seven per cent of cases were in response to temporary illness of the carer; and 13 per cent to allow for a holiday (Lovelock, 1981).

Not all care attendant schemes have such a strong carer focus. In some, the principal aim is to facilitate hospital discharge, or simply to enable a highly dependent person to continue living in the community. In the Liverpool Intensive Domiciliary Care Scheme, for example, the service was designed for unsupported elderly mentally infirm people (Crosby et al., 1983, 1986). In such schemes, the prevention of institutional care tends to be a particularly highly regarded outcome. The Greenwich care attendant scheme illustrates the mixed use that is increasingly common; in 32 cases, the disabled person was the main client, as opposed to eight cases where help was provided for reasons of carer relief (Crossthwaite, 1989).

The client groups covered also vary. Crossroads still caters mainly for the carers of younger physically disabled people, though their work has been extended to the supporters of mentally handicapped people. Bristow and Brenig-Jones's evaluation of the Wirral scheme discusses the consequences of such an extension (Bristow and Brenig-Jones, 1984). In general, the carers of mentally handicapped people were found to be in as great need of care relief as those of the physically disabled. Although the actual care required was similar, it was requested by the carers of mentally handicapped people in a slightly different pattern: less frequently and on a more occasional basis. It was unclear in the study whether this related to the relatively greater availability of forms of day care for mentally handicapped people, for example, through the adult training centres; or to the perceptions or inhibitions of the carers.

The emphasis on younger disabled people is characteristic of the care attendant schemes in general. The three Hampshire schemes described by Lovelock in 1981 were restricted to the younger physically disabled (though subsequent developments in the county have extended the schemes to elderly people (Lovelock, 1985)). The Redbridge scheme described by Hopper and Roberts included mentally disabled people, but excluded those whose primary disability, whether mental or physical, resulted from old age. It should be noted, however, that even where 'the elderly' are excluded, the majority of people helped in these schemes tend to be, following the general pattern of disability, in the older age groups: for example, at Redbridge 76 per cent were over 50.

The bias in the schemes, at least to the *relatively* younger client groups, is largely explicable in terms of the resource consequences of extending provision to elderly people and their carers. Such an extension also raises issues of the integration of care attendant schemes, or those at least that are statutory in their basis, into the mainstream home care service. We shall return to this below.

Turning now to the evaluation of such schemes, the principal work has been by Lovelock (1981), Bristow (1981, 1986), Cooper (1985, 1986), Smith (1986) and Crossthwaite (1989). All include data, whether from interviews or questionnaires, concerning the views of carers of the impact of the service. Most reportage is concerned with the benefits of the service to the carers themselves, though two other areas of outcome measure are also frequently mentioned: the ability of the service to allow a carer to work and the prevention of institutionalisation.

Bristow analysed the comments of carers concerning the impact of the service into nine broad categories. The most frequently mentioned benefit (52 per cent of cases) was in terms of freedom for the carer, followed by peace of mind (39 per cent). Just over a quarter mentioned the relief from physical strain, and relief from emotional strain was mentioned by about the same proportion (26 per cent). A significant number praised the high standard of care the attendant was able to give to their dependant (12 per cent). For eight per cent, the service enabled them to go to work. Two per cent believed the service prevented what would otherwise be an inevitable breakdown (Bristow, 1986). Lovelock's study produced parallel evidence, though the categories used are slightly different.

A similarly positive estimation of the service is reported in Farnsworth's evaluation of the Cheltenham scheme. Here, 83 per cent of carers said that the scheme enabled them to do things they could not do prior to receiving the help. Eighty per cent believed the scheme had improved their quality of life. When asked what they did when the attendant was helping, the most popular category was simply 'relaxing', followed by shopping and going to work (Farnsworth, 1986).

Certain features of the schemes were particularly highly valued. Of these, probably the most significant is flexibility. As Osborne comments:

> what is needed is a service which will mirror the help required by the individuals or his or her carer, rather than the individual having to fit in with an existing statutory service which does not provide what they really need. (preface to Bristow, 1981, p. iii)

The work of care attendants is not task defined, but is modelled on the range and pattern of support that is characteristic of the informal sector. This feature is of central importance in the capacity of schemes both to support dependent people and to support and substitute for their carers. Lovelock's study confirms the variety of tasks performed by attendants and suggests that this range is an indication of the ways in which the service is able to respond to the actual needs of specific situations.

Timing is also clearly crucial. Tasks are not simply cumulative, but have to be performed at particular times. Punctuality is of the essence in any help that aims to substitute for the presence of the carer. These are areas where it is vital that the carer is able to control his or her situation. And it is here that the contrast is most vividly made with statutory services, which are too often limited in their hours of operation and appear inclined to give, in their cancellations and re-schedulings, too great an emphasis to internal service considerations rather than to the interests of carers.

These features of the service are as important, Osborne argues, as the extent of the input:

> Contrary to what many professionals believe, . . . support only has to be in very small amounts, so long as it is reliable, ongoing, given at times required by the relatives, and seen to be there in an emergency. (Osborne, 1981, p.60)

Cooper, writing from the budget-conscious standpoint of a service developer, concurs with this view that 'relatively small amounts of the right type of help have a massive impact on the ability to keep going' (Cooper, 1986, p.25).

The majority of evaluations in this area do not attempt to go beyond gathering the views of carers concerning the impact and benefits of services. Cooper's study did attempt to go further in that it included a joint assessment of a sample of cases in which two professionals were asked to assess both the main functions performed by Crossroads in each case and 'whether it would make professional or financial sense to replace Crossroads with existing statutory services operating within current resource constraints, policy guidelines and priorities?'

The relief of the stress of caring was confirmed to be the main function of the schemes. When asked whether statutory services could replace Crossroads, given the nature of the families' problems, it was found that in two-thirds of the cases:

> not only is Crossroads providing the help wanted by these families, but there is no conceivable substitute from within the statutory services.

Furthermore:

> In a number of cases the joint assessment confirmed that 'the situation would have irrevocably broken down without the input of Crossroads. (Cooper, 1986, p. 25)

One of the potential areas of difficulty with such voluntary schemes concerns the question of substitution. A number of the schemes explicitly aim not to substitute for mainstream home help and nursing services. But there clearly is a potential overlap, and it remains uncertain how far care attendant schemes provide support additional to that of these services, as opposed to instead of them. Judgements as to the appropriateness of such substitution effects also vary. Crossroads, representing the interests of carers who are heavily burdened and who often receive very little or nothing in the way of formal support, regard their service as additional and different. But many schemes are supported by joint finance, and the desire for substitution effects, certainly against health service resources, is an inevitable concomitant of such finance.

Cooper is careful in his evaluation to model the costs of comparable services and not to fall into the trap of an imperfect substitution, whereby the cost of the care attendant scheme is compared with that

of the fairly minimal statutory services for which its more comprehensive support might substitute. Taking this as the basis,
Cooper concludes that the cost of establishing substitute services
would be in the order of double the cost of the Crossroads schemes.

Most schemes as currently operated are small in scale and organised
within the voluntary sector, though perhaps funded by money from
the statutory sector. The evaluations of Lovelock, Bristow and
Crossthwaite all emphasise the benefits of such small-scale enter-
prises in terms of service responsiveness and organisational sensi-
tivity. Any expansion of coverage inevitably raises the familiar
problems of the implementation on a larger scale of successful small
innovations. Crosby et al. in particular questioned the capacity of
local authority schemes to operate as effectively, and particularly
cost-effectively, as voluntary ones (Crosby et al., 1983), a view
confirmed by Cooper's analysis. The question of comparative costs
does, however, raise other issues concerning the employment terms
and levels of wages commonly offered in such schemes. Leat and
Gay (1987) and Thornton (1989) have discussed more fully some of
the problems raised by this grey area between employment and
voluntary work; in particular, questions of 'exploitation', accounta-
bility and responsibility, especially legal responsibility. Thornton
points to the importance of recognising the motivations and rewards
of volunteers, and argues these may put limitations on the degree to
which such flexible voluntary work can be routinised within the
formal system. These reservations apply as much to some of the
respite care schemes that are described later in this review as to the
care attendant schemes. Indeed, as we shall see, there is a
considerable overlap in their functions.

Home care services

The approach adopted by care attendant schemes is not confined to
the voluntary sector. There are obvious parallels between the role of
the care attendant and some of the recent developments within the
home help, increasingly home care, service. This is particularly the
case where the service has adopted the hybrid worker model
whereby a single home care aide, incorporating the tasks of home
help and nursing auxiliary, provides domestic and personal care
support. The recent reports of the Social Services Inspectorate (1987,
1988) discuss the moves towards a home care model within the home
help service. Some of the issues around personal care and the
boundaries of tasks are analysed by Twigg (forthcoming); and Ferlie
(forthcoming) discusses service development models. In general,

these developments tend to be contained within specialist sub-sections of the service, sometimes organised quite separately from the home help service and often supported by joint finance. In a small but increasing number of local authorities, these more flexible roles have been fully integrated within the home care service.

The boundary of tasks performed in the new home care service is frequently defined in terms of those activities that a caring relative would undertake. This definition does not, however, necessarily suggest any substitution for the informal sector. There is as yet no evidence as to the pattern of allocation in such services. It seems likely, particularly given the emphasis on the prevention of institutionalisation that often underpins such schemes, that provision will mirror that of the home help service and be targeted predominantly at those living alone. They are, if anything, less likely to be available to support carers than are the care attendant schemes.

Medical services

The work of the home care service and the care attendant schemes overlaps to some degree with that of the community nursing service, for community nursing operates at the point of transition between what can be seen as assistance with practical tasks often performed by the carer and the more technical forms of medical intervention. These technical forms of intervention, though focused on the dependent patient, can be of central importance for the carer also. We have already noted how the close interdependence of carer and cared-for means that all forms of support to the cared-for are potentially relevant to the situation of the carer. Many carers place high quality medical care as among the most important forms of support, for it has a dual role to play, both directly in potentially reducing levels of physical disability and thus dependence, and less directly in alleviating the anxieties of carers, enabling them to feel that all that can be done for their dependant has been done.

The importance for carers of high quality medical support applies widely. There is a range of medical interventions, from general practitioner support to the specialist services at the hospital, that are relevant. The tradition of medicine is, however, individualistic, focused on the individual patient who is here the dependent person, and not the carer. The sharpness of this focus on the dependant has consequences for the way carers, or as they are more commonly and significantly termed in this medical context 'relatives', are perceived.

Although the importance of relatives and the support they give has been recognised in medical literature, little attention has as yet been given directly to the impact of medical services on these carers.

Even less attention has been given to the impact of the systematic assumptions made by medical professionals about carers and their availability. These assumptions clearly feed into patterns of organisation and resource allocation that have important consequences for carers. Again, there is no major research work to report. One of the few documents that attempts to discuss these issues is *Doctors, Carers and General Practitioners* (Davies, 1989). This presents a programme for use in workshops with general practitioners.

The community nursing service

Not all the tasks performed by community nurses are of a specialist medical character. Much of the potential relevance of the community nursing service for carers lies in its ability to help with the more mundane care tasks, many of which are commonly performed by the carers themselves. As we have noted, the carer's role is a diffuse and comprehensive one. Whereas different sorts of task in the formal system are in general performed by different personnel, all tasks, except the most technical medical ones, are performed by informal carers; though it appears at times that carers even undertake supportive tasks that are otherwise regarded as exclusively the work of a trained nurse. Oliver quotes the example of a carer – his wife – who was informed by a nurse that her husband could not be as disabled as she suggested since such a level of disability required the skilled input of two nurses (Oliver, 1988).

Although the community nursing service plays a potentially important role in the support of carers, there is an almost total lack of evaluative work in the area. Indeed there is still too little systematic information about the degree of involvement of nurses with informal carers though Arber et al's reanalysis of the General Household Survey (see below) offers a number of pointers.

Work with supporting relatives is generally recognised as part of the community nurse's role. This has particularly been the case with the growth of whole-person approaches such as that exemplified in the 'nursing process'. But how extensive such involvement actually is remains unclear, and there are in practice countervailing tendencies that limit its impact. The principal of these are the concept of skilled nursing activity, and the pressure of acute nursing tasks. Unpublished evidence from the Domiciliary Care Project at the University of Kent (Bebbington et al., 1986) suggests that a majority of a sample of community nurse managers saw general supportive tasks such as sitting with a patient while a carer popped to the shops either as clearly not a nursing task or as effectively ruled out by other demands on time. Although the nurse managers expressed support for a whole-person approach to assessment that would include the needs of carers, they did not in practice support whole-person forms of provision, at least by nurses.

The principle grey area remains that of personal care. Personal care tasks, unlike the more diffuse supportive activities referred to above, are clearly recognised as nursing tasks, but in a slightly ambivalent way. They are nursing tasks, but they are not skilled nursing tasks. They do not require a trained nurse and can be performed by an auxiliary or, of course, by a carer. Personal care tasks are constituted less in terms of medical skills than in terms of aspects of intimacy. Personal care involves touching, nakedness, contact with excreta. Its negotiation by nurses appeals, therefore, more to the social construction of a neutral intimacy than to professional skills per se (Twigg, forthcoming). Personal care tasks are recognised as appropriate to nurses, but are not given priority. They exist in the discretionary, grey area of work and are easily displaced by other forms of activity.

Arber et al. (1988) in their analysis of the 1980 General Household Survey found that, as with the allocation of home help, there were systematic patterns of provision of community nursing support that reflected these characteristics of personal care. The patterns of provision related to features of the carer and the dependant, in particular the interaction between the gender of the carer and the gender of the cared for:

> District nursing is twice as likely to be provided where the unmarried adult carer is caring for an elderly person of the opposite sex . . . suggesting that the cultural taboos about opposite sex personal health care operate primarily where the caring is between sexes *and* between generations. (p.169)

The marital status of the carer was once again found to be significant:

> elderly who are co-resident with younger married women are least likely to receive district nursing services . . . . . Thus, married women are more likely to perform the tasks of district nurses than carers living in another type of household. (p. 170)

Beyond this, there appears to be considerable local, indeed individual, variability in provision (Twigg, forthcoming). Support with personal care tasks can be theoretically available, but only episo-dically provided. There is rarely clear information locally as to whether such a service is available and for whom.

This pattern of provision poses considerable problems for carers. Because nurses tend to give priority to acute medical needs, 'maintenance' care is fitted in as it can be. Carers cannot always rely on a nurse to come at a particular time or even on a particular day (Badger et al., 1989). The hours that the community nursing service works also tend to be restricted (Creek et al., 1987). All these are factors that limit the relevance of the service from the carer's point of view. Carers cannot rely on nurses to act as substitutes in such tasks as getting the dependent person up, dressed and to the toilet. They cannot be sure that a nurse will come to give a bath that week.

As a result, though the community nursing service has great potentiality for supporting carers, and those carers who do receive its help are often full of its praise, the reality of its impact appears to be more limited. Robinson believes strongly in the potentiality of nurses in this field (Robinson, 1988), though she recognises the countervailing forces that inhibit such developments.

Respite care

The unrelenting character of much caregiving has been repeatedly described (Nissel and Bonnerjea, 1982; Glendinning, 1983; Levin et al., 1983; Wright, 1986). It is not simply the extent and repetitiveness of the caregiving tasks that can cause distress, but the limitations it places on life as a whole. Robinson and Thurnher (1979), for example, report in a sample of carers of elderly people how the actual activities of caregiving were found less burdensome than the restrictions on personal freedom imposed by the caregiving regime. The Domiciliary Care Project at PSSRU similarly found an association between levels of stress and restrictedness (Bebbington et al., 1986). Studies by Lovelock (1985) and Stephens and Christianson (1986) also point to restrictedness in life as one of the major sources of carer distress. Respite care is offered both as a relief from the 'daily grind' of caregiving, and as an opportunity for the carers to have some time for themselves.

There are a number of services that can be seen as having such a respite function. They vary quite considerably, however, in the degree to which they regard this as central or merely ancillary to their main activity which is most often focused on the dependent person.

Day care

Day care has a number of aims, most of which relate to the client or patient. The support of informal carers is, however, often included among those aims.

Day care is offered in a variety of forms. It can encompass aspects of the work of day hospitals, whether they concentrate on psychiatric or more directly physical problems. It can be provided in Part III or other residential homes. It can take place in designated day centres. These in turn vary greatly in their quality and level of resources. Some are purpose-built and full-time; others are only sessional, poorly equipped and occupy temporary settings such as parish halls that are used for other purposes in the week. As yet still only on a small scale, day care is also being provided by some local authorities and voluntary agencies in the homes of paid volunteers (Williams and Francis, 1988). Some centres, perhaps the majority, are provided by social services; others by the voluntary sector, particularly the voluntary sector as it is related to particular disease or dependency groups. Some centres care for specialist client groups like elderly mentally infirm or blind people; others are generic, or at least officially so, for there tend in practice to be certain patterns of allocation that distinguish among dependent groups. Drawing the line between day care centres and other forms of day provision is not always easy. This is particularly the case with the younger disabled or mentally handicapped adults where the boundary between day centres and ATCs or sheltered workshops, though administratively clear, is more vague as to aims. Similarly with mentally ill or elderly people, the boundaries of day care and drop-in centres, social or lunch clubs can be blurred in terms of purpose at least. Allocation is usually regarded as the defining feature, but it is not always sensible to make such a distinction, and some centres have a mix of allocated and free places. Above all, the content of the service and the nature of the regimes vary, and the character of these are not always made the subject of explicit description. Carter's study provides a review of the range of provision (Carter, 1981).

Five studies in relation to day care have included significant evaluative material regarding its impact on the carers: the studies of Gilleard et al. (1984) and Smith and Cantley (1985) of psychogeriatric day hospitals; Evans et al's study of a travelling day hospital (1986); Fennell et al's study of day centres for elderly people (1981), and the work of Levin et al. in relation to the supporters of elderly mentally infirm people (1983).

We shall first describe briefly the three main forms of day care provision: in day hospitals, in residential homes and in day centres.

We shall then draw out some of the conclusions that emerge from the evaluative work in relation to carers.

Day care in day hospitals

Day hospitals are a service development that has grown out of the demands of acute and geriatric medicine. They offer a potentially more efficient and effective setting for medical care than that provided in out-patient or acute and geriatric ward settings. From this essentially therapeutic focus, many day hospitals have extended their role to include general social support for long-term patients and, with that, support for their care-giving relatives.

Day hospitals vary considerably in the degree to which such developments are openly part of their policy. Critics like Murphy argue that such developments are both an inappropriate use of health care resources – 'day hospitals should be treating medical conditions not providing social support' – and an inadequate response to social needs – 'Aren't they just rather bad day centres with drugs?' (Murphy, 1985).

The undefined character of the aims of many day hospitals and the discretionary role of clinicians in their operation make it hard to assess how extensively such units are indeed involved in providing purely 'social' care and, with that, respite support for carers. The availability of day hospital places in a district cannot be interpreted in any simple way as indicating provision for the relief of carers.

It is in the area of psychiatric, especially psychogeriatric, care that day hospitals have chosen to adopt a more openly carer-oriented, respite role. This is clear from the study of four psychogeriatric day hospitals undertaken by Gilleard et al. where relief to the carer was regarded as a major benefit of attendance.

Smith and Cantley's study similarly identifies the carers as the main potential beneficiaries of the day hospital:

> Overall, relatives point to relief by custodial care as being the main benefit derived from the hospital. (p.143)

This benefit had, however, to be seen in the light of certain limitations. These will be discussed at the end of this section, since many of the issues they raise apply to day care in general.

Day care in residential homes

A second major venue for day care is in residential homes. Here the respite or custodial aspects appear to be prominent. The level of resources and facilities made available to day attenders in homes are often so poor that the rationale of the service is largely in terms of carer relief.

Provision is fragmented. Allen's study (1983), however, suggests that places are relatively widely available through the country, although not in great numbers. It is not clear from the study what the overall pattern of pressure on provision is, or whether the relative lack of pressure in some areas indicates an unpopularity in the service. Certainly, anecdotal evidence suggests that this is the case. Allen does express quite considerable concern about the quality and appropriateness of this form of provision, pointing to the lack of explicit activity centred on day attenders, and the relatively alienating character of the experience.

One advantage that day care in residential homes does offer is long hours. Homes can potentially look after a dependent person throughout the day and into the evening, whereas the truncated day offered at many day centres is, as we shall see, a major limitation for some carers. Day care in homes can from the point of view of carers, be a more flexible and responsive form of provision, and this underlies the small but growing use of day care in the private residential sector. There is as yet no systematic study of such provision. Weaver, Willcocks and Kellaher (1985) found, however, that some 13 per cent of private homes in Norfolk provided day care.

Day care at day centres
Lastly, the most common form of day care is in day centres. Such centres vary in the degree to which they regard the support or relief of carers as a central aim. In general, this aspect is more to the fore the more disabled, particularly mentally disabled, the attender is. Carter (1981), looking at a wide range of day units, found only 14 per cent of heads of units regarded carer relief as an important aspect of their provision. But among centres for the confused elderly, 50 per cent of heads saw carer relief as the main aim. (Whether these figures would now be higher in the light of the greater interest in carer issues today is an open question.)

The link between mental disability and a carer focus is clearly borne out in many descriptions of day care initiatives for elderly mentally infirm people, where respite for carers is regarded as the central activity and where a number of support services for carers – groups, advice, etc – are built around that core. Watt (1982), Farries (1985) and Doyle and Hunt (1985) provide examples of such integrated, carer-orientated services. This model of using day care as a focus around which to group a more general support for carers is a feature also of a number of psychogeriatric day hospitals (Keegan, 1984; Smith and Cantley, 1985).

The impact of day care

Turning now to the evaluation of such provision, there is clear evidence of the benefit derived by carers from day care.

Wright in her study of the carers of elderly parents reported a positive response, at least among the small number of carers who had experience of the service. One daughter reported:

> I would go mad if it wasn't for the day centre. She goes there three times a week. Really I could not have stuck it if she didn't go there . . . I know she can't help it, but she has got so irritating since the stroke. She does everything wrong and so slowly. (Wright, 1986, p.145)

In general, this favourable estimation is echoed in other descriptive work (Keegan, 1984).

The role of day care appears to be particularly significant for those looking after someone with dementia. Levin in her study of the supporters of elderly mentally infirm people regarded day care as a 'key component' in the support of this group (Levin, et al., 1983). The carers interviewed placed a high value on day care and emphasised in particular the ways in which it allowed them to get on with tasks, typically shopping, that they were otherwise prevented from doing. It did not, however, help greatly in allowing them to pursue a social life.

Gilleard et al. (1984) in their study of four psychogeriatric day hospitals also found that carers reported benefits to themselves and that these benefits increased over time. These positive carer outcomes were not, however, correlated with any greater tendency for the elderly person to continue living in the community; Gilleard et al. suggest that carers' perceptions of benefit and the maintenance of community care should be regarded as quite separate outcome domains. The lack of correlation was partly explained by the nature of the patient group and the inherent frailty of their situations. Gilleard et al. (1984–6), drawing in addition on the work of Greene and Timbury and Jones and Murdoch, comment on the ways in which such units provide an essentially holding function: '50 per cent of admissions had been admitted to institutional care within six months'. But it was a holding operation that was often achieved at the cost of straining families almost beyond endurance.

Fennell et al. (1981) make a similar point in relation to the maintenance in the community of those day centre clients who are on the margins of institutional care. Here, the relief function of day care must be weighed against the costs to relatives of maintaining a situation that is essentially at crisis point. The appropriateness of such intervention should, they argue, be questioned.

Certain other limitations emerge concerning the potential usefulness of day care in supporting carers.

Day care is typically a thinly-spread service. Fennell et al. report how 50 per cent of elderly confused attenders came to the centres for less than three days a week. Thirty per cent did attend for four or five days, but the majority of these were people who lived alone. In Levin's study, 80 per cent of attendances were for less than four days a week.

Similarly restricted are the hours of day care, or as Murphy terms it, 'midday care' (Murphy, 1985). Though some units for elderly mentally infirm people are open seven days a week and for long hours, five days or less and between the hours of 10.30am to 4.00pm are the more standard forms of provision. Such a pattern of availability does not allow a carer to engage in full-time work.

Although day care is widely reported as helpful, it is often not provided frequently enough or for long enough particularly for those who are very heavily burdened. Fennell et al. found that carers valued the break, but that for the heavily stressed its impact on their essential problems was not great. Thompson in her investigation of the demand for respite care (Thompson, 1986) reported similar findings concerning the limitations of a few hours break. This was particularly the case when weighed against the possible fuss and difficulty of getting the dependent person off to the centre.

There are individuals for whom the limited character of day care appears to offer an appropriate and particularly acceptable form of support. Ramdas suggests that this is the case for certain closely involved carers, typically daughters, who do not want their relationship of responsibility disturbed and who value a limited service that occurs outside the home and outside the relationship (Ramdas, 1986). Such patterns of acceptability emphasise yet again the need for assessment of individual carers, their views and situations. This is a point reiterated by Fennell.

It is perhaps in the nature of a service based around activities that take place at a centre or hospital that the lives of the attenders outside that centre should remain rather shadowy. As a result, the specific situations and needs of carers tend not to be in the forefront of the minds of service providers. Considered knowledge of the carer's situation appears far from common. Carter found that despite the expressed aim of carer relief at many centres, this did not result in any planned framework for contact with relatives. Such contacts as there were remained largely ad hoc and infrequent. In a similar way, orientation procedures rarely involved relatives. This impression of the level and quality of contact with carers is repeated in Smith and Cantley's account of the day hospital, where they concluded that visits by carers to the hospital were few and that carers in general had 'very limited conversations' with staff. The impression remains one of a set of service providers whose view is relatively narrowly circumscribed by the boundaries of the centre itself.

Respite care in institutions

A variety of terms are used to describe respite care in institutions: rotational care, planned care, intermittent admissions, phased care. The significance of the different terms relates to the degree to which the provision is regarded as frequent and cyclical or intermittent and ad hoc. The majority of respite care appears to be provided for periods of a week or a fortnight, bookable in advance and mainly used to allow carers to take holidays. In addition to this, some institutions provide relief on a more frequent, cyclical basis, for example offering admission for two weeks in every six. Additional short-term and emergency admissions can sometimes be fitted in.

Care is provided in a variety of venues. In the local authority sector, the majority of short-term care is provided in Part III homes. At the time of Allen's study, over three-quarters of local authorities provided some short-term care in their homes, nearly a third doing so in all their homes (Allen, I., 1983). In about three-quarters of authorities, such beds were set aside specifically for respite, though with some flexibility; in the remaining quarter, beds were organised according to supply and demand. Allen estimated that some 50–60 per cent of such short-term care was provided for reasons of carer relief or holidays. *Care for a Change*, produced by the Social Services Inspectorate (1987a), provides a more recent description of respite services within the personal social services, but it concentrates on examples from only nine agencies and does not attempt to provide a systematic review of practice.

Respite care is also provided in the private residential sector. Once again, there is no systematic data on this, but the Weaver, Willcocks and Kellaher study (1985) found that of private residential homes in Norfolk, some 36 per cent provided short-term care. There have been similar developments within the private nursing home sector where relief care is perceived as an area of potential growth.

Institutionally-based respite care is also available within the health service, as part of the mental handicap, geriatric and psychogeriatric services. It is difficult to quantify the level of this. Some respite is provided in designated beds, mainly on long-stay wards, but other respite is made available at the discretion of the consultant, using ordinary provision.

In addition to such off-shoots of the residential and hospital sectors, respite care has increasingly been provided as a specialist service, often within the voluntary sector. Such developments have also begun to occur within the local authority sector with the development of specialist respite facilities. Developments within the voluntary sector are as yet limited, since the capital and revenue implications are considerable. However, initiatives have begun to emerge such as that of the family support unit set up by the Alzheimer's Disease Society in conjunction with Cleveland Social Services. This provides a resource centre for carers of elderly mentally infirm people, offering a flexible package of day care, evening care and overnight respite care for up to four weeks (Farries, 1985).

The unremitting character of caregiving and the particular strains associated with restrictedness and close and constant contact with a dependant, particularly a mentally confused or behaviourally disturbed dependant, have already been referred to. It is not surprising that those attempts to support carers that have resulted from the initiatives of carers *themselves* have often focused their efforts on the provision of respite care (Crossman, London and Barry, 1981; Thompson, 1986). This emphasis has been repeated in developmental work within the statutory sector. In the London Borough of Sutton, for example, a questionnaire administered to carers as part of the Sutton Carers' Project found strong support for respite care as the 'single most helpful thing that [could] be offered to them' (Pinchin, 1987). As a result, priority was given in the project's work to developing a strategy for respite care.

The favourable estimation of respite care implied by this is borne out in research that has examined its impact on individual carers. Levin found respite care a particularly highly appreciated service; a view repeated in the study by Ramdas. Allen found 'some of the most heartfelt comments' were expressed in relation to the relief it offered (Allen, I., 1983, p.161). Respite was particularly valued by Levin's supporters as a means of enabling social contacts, something the more limited relief of day care was unable to achieve.

These benefits were clearly repeated in objective measures. Among Levin's sample, those caring with the help of respite care and day care (the vast majority of those receiving respite care also had day care) demonstrated a decline in levels of stress between the two interviews; whereas those caring without such support showed an increase.

Parallel reductions in stress scores over a period of only a fortnight were reported by McKay et al. (1983) in relation to the carers of elderly people admitted to a GP hospital for acute care. Simply being away from one's dependant, even for a short period, was clearly beneficial

The evaluation of the Family Support Unit in Cleveland (Donaldson et al., 1988), which provides respite care for the supporters of elderly mentally infirm people, demonstrates – though with some provisos – that the dependants of those who received the support of the unit survived significantly longer in the community than did a matched group of dependants and carers. Because the carers who were supported by the Family Support Unit consumed higher levels of services in general than did the matched control group, the unit cost of their support was greater. If, however, one compares the cost per *extra* day spent in the community of the FSU supported group with the alternative cost of institutional care, the FSU is clearly cost-effective (£18.79 per day compared with £45.72 per day). However, the likely alternatives to the extra days of survival are not solely hospital care, but include also lower-cost forms of support such as residential care, or death without any further consumption of resources. The balance of these could not be predicted, and the evaluation concludes therefore that while there are *indications* of cost-effectiveness these have not been established fully.

In the face of such consensus concerning at least the benefits of respite care, what sense can be made of evidence suggesting a limited take-up of the service? Allen in her study reported that it was 'very rare, however, to hear of people being turned down for short-stay care, and it usually appeared that this was not an oversubscribed resource' (p.28). Thompson in her local survey of the need for respite care draws attention in her sample to high felt need and yet low use of existing respite services (Thompson, 1986).

Thompson believes the answer lies in the experience of caring itself which is isolating, draining and cuts the carer off from word-of-mouth information. Allen concurs with such a view of restricted information and, pointing to the evidence that those who use respite care are a small number who do so frequently, concludes that there is a service network, and that many carers not on that network remain unaware of a form of support that could be a lifeline for them. It appears from the pattern of service use that access to respite care is typically via other forms of service, usually, according to Levin, day care and that those outside this basic service net remain unaware of what is available. Wright similarly emphasises the failure of professionals to inform carers about what is available (Wright, 1986). This, and the fact that access to the facility is more in the control of professionals than is the case with some other services, may contribute to a situation where demand is kept artificially low.

It is clear, however, that the barriers to the take-up of respite care are not only external ones. There are features of institutional respite care as it is currently organised that make it less useful or potentially off-putting for some carers and, indeed, for some of their dependants.

The first of these concerns the pattern of availability. Carers need both planned *and* emergency access to respite care. Ideally, respite beds should be available at short notice not only to meet major crises, but in order to allow carers to take advantage of the opportunities of life that other individuals can accept.

Such a flexible and responsive service is, however, rare. Ramdas remarks on the debilitating delays in the processing of applications for respite care, the lack of explanation of what is going on and the need to badger for the service. It was unclear to many of her respondents exactly how one should apply for such support. Many of these respondents felt that service providers were far too focused on the needs of the elderly person and failed to recognise *their* needs as the central issue for respite care (Ramdas, 1986).

The failure to place the carer at the centre of the service explains much of the difficulty over the inflexible character of respite care. Respite care is too often provided as a sideline in hospitals and residential homes, and is frequently created out of marginal resources within the institutions. As such, it tends to be managed and judged in terms of bed use and through-put. But responsiveness to carers' needs is essentially at odds with such an emphasis on the 'efficient' use of resources. Watson (1983) describing a hospital-based respite service for elderly mentally infirm people, defines 'flexibility' thus:

> There has to be flexibility. This is of utmost important for efficiency and economy. If a bed is empty, for example, the sister will take a discharged patient for a short period to give the relatives a holiday.

So long as services are viewed this way round, as a marginal resource to be allocated when convenient to the institution, true responsiveness to carer needs will remain remote.

Related to these difficulties of service orientation are problems related to the venue of care. It is clear that respite care cannot easily be integrated with other forms of care. This is particularly true of acute hospital care. Work from Australia and the United States, where such patterns of provision are imposed by the constraints of the care system, illustrate the essential unsuitability of acute care settings for respite care. Frank's account of respite care in an Adelaide hospital explores some of the problems of service operation posed by such admissions (Frank, 1984). Hasselkus and Brown's study of a similar scheme in a veteran's hospital in Wisconsin illustrates the difficulties such a venue can cause: 'regression into the sick role . . . rapid loss of strength and diminishing mobility after long hours of inactivity in the hospital room', and the puzzlement of hospital staff 'accustomed to a role geared to acute care and a system of prioritising ward care to meet the needs of the most seriously ill' (Hasselkus and Brown, 1983, p.85).

This rather negative picture of hospital-based care is repeated in the preferences of carers, expressed to Ramdas, who by and large disliked the character of hospital-based care and preferred other forms of respite. The difficulties of integrating respite care into institutions whose main purposes are different are not confined to the hospital sector. Boldy and Kuh conclude that:

> a large home whose primary function is to care for long stay clients is bound to find it hard to respond sensitively to the needs of short-stay clients. In this environment, it seems to be the client – not the home – that responds, for it is the client who must 'fit in'. (Boldy and Kuh, 1984, p.174)

A majority of the homes studied by Allen reported respite admissions to be problematic, and this contrasts with the rather easy assumption of many managers of the benefits to be derived from such a use of resources. Allen concludes that short-stay care is most successful where provided in homes that specialise in such provision.

The second set of difficulties posed by such institutional respite care are more problematic, for they relate to the impact on the dependants themselves. Allen here provides a critique that parallels that of Oswin in relation to the short-term institutional placement of disabled children (Oswin, 1984). There is in particular a lack of understanding of the social experience of such admissions; it is clear from a number of studies (Allen, I., 1983; Levin, 1983; Hasselkus and Brown, 1983; Frank, 1984) that short-term care can in fact increase mental confusion and disorientation. Some carers of people with

Parkinson's Disease, for example, while appreciating the break spoke of 'having to work even harder to "get the patient right" on coming home' (Kelson, 1985).

The problems of transition, the fears of abandonment, the implicit denial of the relationship, the lack of sufficient knowledge of the elderly or disabled person so as to make their stay enjoyable: all contribute to a generally negative experience for the dependent person. As a result, this can lead to feelings of guilt in the carer that can lead him or her to decide not to take up the opportunity of such a break again. Wright reports one such case of deterioration:

> There was no problem with her walking when she went into the geriatric ward but when I got her out two weeks later she could not walk at all. I had to teach her how to walk again. They found her behaviour difficult to cope with and gave her drugs which made her keep in bed the whole time. She lost the use of her legs. It's just not worth it when you have to face that. (p.144)

The generally negative character of the experience is illustrated in the way some heads of homes in Allen's study reported:

> one of the most important advantages to the short-term residents as being to make them more appreciative of life outside the home and to be more grateful and aware of what their carers were doing for them. (p.52)

It is hard to think of a bleaker outcome measure of the effectiveness of respite care.

As a result of these features, many carers feel inhibited about suggesting respite care to their dependant. For some, the difficulties prior to and after admission make the service more trouble than it is worth (Thompson, 1986). Parker in her study of spouse carers analyses the ways in which the use of respite care has to be negotiated between the carer and the cared-for. Whether the dependant agrees to go into respite or not is subject to the dynamics of power in the marital relationship. Not surprisingly, she found that gender and the structured expectations that relate to it played an important role in determining uptake (Parker, 1989).

It is clear from these studies that conflicts of interest between carer and dependant are more starkly presented by respite care than by any other service. The comparison with day care brings this out more clearly. While day care is of benefit, its overall impact appears to be slightly limited and it may not really affect the essential situation of, at least, the heavily burdened. Institutional respite does appear to do this, but at some cost to the dependant.

There is a second sense in which respite care may reveal the conflicts of interest, and this relates to its impact on the willingness of the carer to continue giving care. Certainly, some carers fear that the impact of a real break will be such as to allow them to realise at what personal cost they have been providing care, and they have as a result refused respite care (Ramdas, 1986). The Levin study found an association between respite care and institutionalisation, but whether the association was a causal one remained unclear.

Scharlach and Frenzel (1986) in interviews with 150 carers of disabled American veterans found that 30 per cent reported that experience of respite care made them feel that it was *more* likely that their dependent person would go into institutional care. (Thirty-three per cent felt that it was less likely.)

> Some caregivers reported that the temporary experience of relief made them more aware of what they were sacrificing by giving up so much in their own lives to care for their loved ones. As one caregiver stated: 'I finally realised that he can exist without my constant care'. (Scharlach and Frenzel, 1986)

The sombre truth appears to be that the more the service helps the heavily burdened carer, the less it is likely to benefit the dependent person and it may even cause them some harm. Levin believes despite this, however, that respite care is still a resource of central importance and that any reservations we may have concerning the service should not distract from the need to make it more widely available. Adverse effects, she argues, can be tackled.

There is certainly room for improvement in the ways in which respite care is provided, and Allen's more detailed analysis points to many such aspects of practice that require closer attention. Above all, perhaps the key lies in regarding respite care as a service in itself, rather than as a sideline poorly integrated into what is essentially an institutional provision. Finally, it is important in the face of evidence such as that provided by Scharlach and Frenzel (1986) to remember that the prevention of institutionalisation is not the only aim of respite services. Enabling the carer finally to let go must also be a valid goal.

Family placement and fostering schemes

One form of service that attempts to circumvent the problems caused by institutional respite care is family placement, whereby an elderly or disabled person is 'fostered' or 'boarded out' with a family who typically receive some financial recompense.

Such placements were originally mainly intended to be long-term, but in the last decade, particularly under the influence of the Leeds Family Placement Scheme, there has been a growth in short-term placements. (Simpson and Traynor, 1987) describe the first ten years of the Leeds scheme.)

Thornton and Moore have reviewed some of these developments (Thornton and Moore, 1980). In 1980 they traced 23 such schemes, half of which specialised in short-term placements. Two-thirds of the elderly individuals cared for by schemes usually lived with relatives; though in one Bolton project reported by Keating and Rickett (1982), the proportion was over 80 per cent. Carer relief is thus one of the major functions of such schemes, and over half the placements in the Thornton and Moore study were directly to relieve carers. The majority of placements were for one or two weeks to allow carers to take holidays. Emergency admissions were rare, as was phased care. Thornton and Moore's report contains some comments concerning good practice and effectiveness, but theirs was not essentially an evaluative study. The 1986 report of Newcastle City Council, however, contains an evaluation of its STOP scheme which provides short-term care in a family environment for mentally handicapped adults.

Motives for establishing such schemes are mixed, and frequently contain an assumption, as with the Leeds placement scheme, that fostering offers a particularly cost-effective form of provision; a view that Thornton and Moore believe may be mistaken if the full social work and administrative costs are taken into account. More important is the belief that informal, family-based care is in some sense more 'natural' and that it can avoid many of the well-documented shortcomings of institutional care (Crosby, 1985). Crosby in particular notes the difference between the Leeds scheme and American projects that offer a much more restricted board and lodgings approach. Many of the accounts of such schemes speak warmly of the benefits of a *family* atmosphere; Newton in describing a Liverpool scheme refers to the 'intimate warmth' that it can offer (Newton, 1981). Certainly, Thornton and Moore found that the majority of those elderly people who had experienced a Part III home said they preferred the family placement scheme, which they regarded as providing a more individual and natural setting.

Beyond this, however, in relation to elderly people there is little in the way of directly evaluative work concerning the impact of placements. Reference is made in some accounts to rehabilitation and improved functioning (Keating and Rickett, 1982; Newton,

1981), but this is not examined systematically. Such accounts contrast well with the picture of deterioration associated with some institutional respite care.

In relation to mentally handicapped people, the evaluation of the Newcastle-based STOP scheme found that carers reported that their mentally handicapped offspring had actually benefited from the regular placement (Newcastle City Council, 1986). They were particularly felt to benefit from the broadening of their horizons gained through social contact. There was evidence that the availability of this version of respite had led families to stop using the hospital-based respite facility, though they did continue to use some other versions of respite. Such a pattern does perhaps suggest a process of voting with one's feet. And it is indicative, once again, of some of the problems that can attach to institutional versions of respite care.

Reviewing the sources of the scheme's success, the Newcastle report emphasises in particular its flexibility, and identifies this flexibility with a series of factors. These include among others: the initial matching of helper and family, followed by their freedom to make their own arrangements as to the most suitable form of care; linked to this, the facilitating rather than the dominating role of the scheme's staff; and the needs-based form of assessment. It is this flexibility, the report concludes, that is 'a most dramatic point of contrast with traditional hospital respite care'. The report does, however, face up to what it also identifies as the major limitation in the flexibility of the approach. This concerns the ways in which the matching process of helpers to families is based around the choice of the helper, so that 'some potential users of family respite care will never receive it because no [helpers] will spontaneously arise to provide them with a service' (Newcastle City Council, 1986, p.52). This has proved to be more of a problem with STOP than it has with the parallel scheme, termed FACE, that caters for mentally handicapped children.

This in turn raises a more general point concerning the types of dependent people for whom such schemes cater. It is hard to examine this systematically in the absence of detailed breakdowns. There is, however, some indication that the clients of such schemes tend to be less dependent, or confused, or behaviourally disturbed than those of institutional schemes.

Turning more directly to the views of carers, the Newcastle study found 79 per cent of families using the scheme were 'very satisfied' and 13 per cent were 'satisfied', but it did not go beyond this rather simple measure of effectiveness. In general, there is less discussion of the impact of the service on carers than one might expect, and, for example, little exploration of the problems carers might face in accepting a service based around a rival family whose willingness to care might be interpreted as a rebuke to theirs. In contrast to this possibility, however, there are a number of references to a spontaneous relationship developing between the temporary carer and the dependant and his or her family that extended beyond the care period (Keating and Rickett, 1982; Crosby, 1985).

Sitter and other home relief services

Sitter and other home relief schemes provide a form of service that brings respite care into the carer's own home by providing individuals who will sit with an elderly or dependent person. Some schemes are limited to such a 'sitter' role, providing company, surveillance and minor forms of assistance. But in many schemes, perhaps the majority, the helper or worker acts essentially as a substitute for the carer, performing the supportive tasks that are normally undertaken by the carer. Such helpers or workers may often be involved in domestic and personal care work. In a similar way, a number of the care attendant schemes, particularly Crossroads Care, combine their care substitution work with a respite function. There is thus a certain artificiality in attempting to separate out these forms of support. Thornton provides a review of the range of provision in this area which she extends to include the care assistant schemes (Thornton, 1989a).

Typically such schemes are organised within the voluntary sector, though sometimes with Manpower Services Commission, now Department of Employment, money (Hodge, 1987) or joint funding. They are often established as part of a more general strategy, for example, to support elderly mentally infirm people and their carers, that can include day care and a resource centre. The Nottingham Family Support Service (Mullender, 1983) and the Bristol Support the Elderly Mentally Infirm Scheme (Moore, 1985) provide examples of such combinations. Other sitter schemes have put together the needs of carers of elderly and dependent people with those of single parents (Triseliotis, 1985; Hodge, 1987). Some schemes, for example the In Safe Hands Project organised by Age Concern in York, provide a variety of forms of respite support that include sitting, fostering and staying in the dependent person's house (Cowen and Johnson, 1985; Thornton, 1989a). Such schemes are able to offer a flexible service as the circumstances of the carer and cared-for change.

Hours available to carers vary, as does uptake. Some carers use the service relatively intensively to enable them to engage in paid work;

others for a very limited number of outings, perhaps to the hospital (Southampton MIND, 1984). There is evidence that many schemes operate restrictions on the amount of help that any one carer may receive (Thornton, 1989a). This can limit their usefulness for certain sorts of carer, for example, those who wish to work, though it may enable a greater number of carers to receive help. A number of schemes also operate with extensive waiting lists.

The majority of schemes provide relief during the day. While night sitting is available, it tends to be a minor part of the service, and it is more typically associated with paid rather than unpaid voluntary helpers (Thornton, 1989a).

Many services require some payment by the carers; some carers report finding this formal, monetary relation helpful (Moore, 1985). In some cases, the fees are set at token levels. Schemes vary in regard to the payment of helpers. Some schemes employ helpers on an hourly care-assistant rate, others provide more limited payments, while others rely on voluntary labour. The issues around payment are explored in greater detail by Leat and Gay (1987) and by Thornton (1989a).

Many schemes offer some form of training. Carers valued this training, or the knowledge that sitters had personal experience of caregiving. The voluntary services also appear to attract a number of experienced and even formally-trained volunteers, such as ex-nurses.

Respite provided in this way offers, potentially, the least disruptive form of service. This is true both for the dependent person who is not required to go into a strange environment, and for the carer who is not required to organise and get their dependant out of the house. Thompson, in particular, endorses the importance of relief care in the home. In doing so, she draws on personal experience, both as a social worker and informal carer, of the ways in which social services, as she regards it, pluck people from their natural environments and relegate relatives to marginal roles (Thompson, 1986).

It is a solution that may not suit all carers. Ramdas found carers who felt their sense of territoriality disturbed by the idea and who were unhappy at the thought of having a stranger come into their home (Ramdas, 1986). It should be noted, however, that these were individuals who had not directly experienced the service. Whether their views would be modified had they done so remains uncertain. One of the general problems of exploring the views of carers about services is that many carers have experienced so little in the way of support services that their comments can be dominated by perceptions of the imagined problems posed in receiving the service.

Another group for whom home respite is of limited value are carers who do not want to go *out*, but want time for themselves in their own homes.

Two other categories of carer have been identified in some of the accounts of sitter schemes as reluctant in their uptake: these were families at the early stages of care responsibility, suggesting once again the difficulties of getting carers to regard themselves as eligible for services, or services as appropriate for them; and carers whose relationship to caregiving and its strains was such that they could not relinquish the burden. The voluntary and 'optional' character of sitter services may mean that they are less successful in breaking through carer reluctance than services which are assigned by professionals.

The benefits to the dependant of such home-based schemes are apparent not only in their avoidance of some of the detrimental effects associated with institutional respite care, but in some actual gains for the dependant. Moore notes in relation to a sample of elderly mentally infirm people that:

> it was not foreseen that the service would have such a beneficial effect on the sufferers. They were provided with companionship, stimulation, and the opportunity for more responsive behaviour. The therapeutic aspect of regular visits by a caring person with the energy to provide and promote new experiences has been a bonus. (Moore, 1985, p.13)

Similar social benefits were reported, particularly in relation to forms of physical dependency like hemiplegia, in other schemes (Robinson and Luszczak, 1986).

With regard to the carers themselves, however, it may be the case that sitter services, at least where provided for relatively short periods of time, are subject to the same limitations as day care: that they provide a helpful break but one whose duration is too short to affect fundamentally the situation of the heavily burdened. How far this is the case is difficult to assess since so few of the schemes have undertaken any evaluation, even at the simple level of asking carers about the impact of the scheme. Thus Triseliotis in quite a long report of a sitter service states : 'the families themselves were not asked to formulate how they had benefited from the service' (p.61). Thornton in her study of the In Safe Hands Scheme in York did interview the carers, and recounts a strongly positive response; she explains how the way in which the service was organised and delivered appeared to add to the value of the break itself (Thornton, 1989a).

The review of the scheme set up by Southampton MIND also interviewed the carers and the account reports:

> while demonstrating some ambiguity between their need for relief and their guilt about such a need, none voiced any doubts as to the help the sitting service had been to them. (Southampton MIND, 1984)

In addition, there is evidence that some carers gained from their social contact with the sitters who were able to provide companionship, interest and support (Southampton MIND, 1984).

The question of the relationship between the carer and the sitter raises an important point concerning the constraints on the use of volunteers in this area. A number of the sitter services are aimed at supporting elderly mentally infirm people. This is a client group for whom the appropriateness of using volunteers has been questioned. May, McKeganey and Flood (1986) have analysed the failure of one voluntary visiting scheme. A number of factors contributed to its failure, but among these was the clear difficulty of relating to an elderly mentally infirm person and the lack of positive reinforcement of the volunteer's sense of worth. (The volunteers were supporting the elderly people and not their carers.) May, McKeganey and Flood argue that such interpersonal reward is an essential element in the successful use of volunteers. By contrast, the sitter services provided to support carers do appear to be able to mobilise sitter support for elderly mentally infirm people. The Southampton MIND account, for example, reports no problem in using untrained people, but goes on to elaborate one of the reasons:

> When their attitudes to the job were discussed at a group meeting they expressed the view that the relationship they built up with the carer, and the knowledge of how they were relied upon by the carers, helped them to accept the demands and frustrations of looking after psychogeriatric patients. (Southampton MIND, 1984, p.801)

It is clear therefore that the relationship between the carer and the sitter is vital both for the benefits it can bring to the carer and for the reinforcement it gives the sitters. It is an essential element in such schemes, particularly where dealing with elderly mentally infirm people.

Case management approaches

So far, the focus of this review has been on a series of discrete services. Some of these services in fact offer a range of support, and many would emphasise the flexibility that that range of response gives them. This is particularly the case with the care attendant schemes and with other projects that provide the services of a 'composite' worker who will perform a variety of supportive tasks.

But, as important to carers as these individual services or schemes are the ways in which services are put together. Carers and their dependants often have a variety of needs for which no single service alone is appropriate. Furthermore, carers – if they receive the levels of support they need for themselves and their dependants – often find themselves at the centre of a complex pattern of service delivery in which no single figure has the responsibility for the assessment, management and co-ordination of the package as a whole.

These difficulties are not confined to the area of carer support, but are familiar in the co-ordination and provision of care generally. Two elements stand out: first, the problem of assessment, and particularly assessment for need rather than assessment for services; and second, the problems of both intra- and inter-agency co-ordination, with the related issues of control over the allocation of resources.

It is in the context of these problems that case management has increasingly been seen as a way forward. Case management is an integrated approach to care provision in which a single case manager controls access to the provision of a number of services and has an overall responsibility to meet the needs of the client. Davies and Challis (1986) describe the five core tasks of case management as: case finding, assessment, care planning, service arrangement and monitoring. Most of the case management literature originates from the United States, where its role is underwritten by the organisational division between agencies that assess and agencies that contract to deliver care. The approach is, however, increasingly being applied to the British situation. Case management involves in many senses a refinement and extension of a role already familiar in social work. The Gloucester Care for Elderly People at Home Project (Dant et al., 1989) employs a case management approach. Perhaps the best known application is that of the Kent Community Care Scheme and the series of replications of it undertaken by the Personal Social Services Research Unit. Davies and Challis (1986) and Challis and Davies (1986) provide evaluations of the Kent scheme and review its background.

In the Kent project, case managers were provided with budgets, set at two-thirds the cost of a residential home place, with which to assess and arrange for the provision of individual packages of care for their frail elderly clients. In addition to ordinary services, case managers were free to use the budget to pay for community care helpers or to mobilise other forms of community resource.

The Kent-derived schemes are concerned with providing support to frail elderly people in the community. As such, they are not centrally carer support schemes. They do, however, recognise the importance of informal carers both as a form of resource that should be fostered and supported, and as individuals whose well-being is properly part of the concern of such schemes. Challis and Davies suggest, in line with other work, that for services to meet carers' needs more effectively requires:

> sensitive professional assessment, greater appropriateness of services to individual needs and greater influence of carers in the decision about the nature and type of care. (Challis and Davies, p. 117)

This, they argue, is what the Kent model of case management is able to offer.

Challis, Luckett and Chessum describe the aims of the approach in the Gateshead version of the project as:

> to complement help already available in the community and offer realistic and meaningful relief so as to consolidate informal care, rather than undermine it. (Challis et al., 1983)

There are two ways in which the Kent model involves the informal sector. These are sometimes confused by commentators. The first involves the recruitment of 'helpers' from the informal sector. These can be neighbours or newly recruited volunteers. They do receive some financial payments, though these are individually negotiable. They belong, therefore, to that quasi-informal sector that has been examined in another context by Leat and Gay. Much of the effectiveness of the scheme lies in its capacity to blur the distinction between the formal and the informal sectors, drawing on the flexibility and emotional responsiveness of the informal sector while focusing and co-ordinating its efforts.

The second sense – and the one that concerns this review – is in the involvement of the schemes in supporting informal carers. Part of this work can extend to the co-ordination and negotiation of existing care networks so as to achieve the optimal pattern of support:

This may mean persuading them to alter what they do and when they do it, to increase their input, or place more realistic limits on it so as to improve the quality and reliability of care without interfering unreasonably in the lives and relationships of others, or displacing their caring roles. (Challis et al., 1983)

In some small number of cases (three in the Kent version), informal carers were co-opted into the scheme as helpers. This involved their receiving some payment for the support they gave to their relatives, but in the context of helping other clients in addition. These cases were rare and reflected particular circumstances. In general, the PSSRU model does not open up the way to employing carers.

The evaluation of the Kent scheme demonstrates a number of favourable outcomes in relation to carers. Taking the example of service receipt, case management appears to result in higher levels of mobilisation than was the case with matched individuals receiving the 'normal' version of services. The level of provision of home help, for example, for clients with carers involved was much closer to the pattern that applies where no carer is involved; the home help service typically being targeted on those who live alone. This suggests that the approach is one that rather than 'exploiting' carers enhances the levels of indirect support that they receive.

In relation to outcomes directly related to the well-being of the carer, which are regarded in the evaluation as forms of final outcome, the scheme again displayed favourable results. On three variables – subjective burden, extent of strain and mental health difficulties – the differences between the community care and comparison groups were significant. The small number of cases made such differences difficult to trace in detail; however, the primary impact of the project on carers appeared to be in the areas of the relief of stress and subjective burden. In interpreting this pattern, Challis and Davies point in particular to the role of the case manager in relieving the anxieties of relatives that can result from the sense of total responsibility. They also point to the more closely tailored emotional and practical support that workers were able to offer.

Lastly, the community care scheme did not appear to undermine or substitute for informal care:

indeed it appeared that carers were if anything less likely to reduce their support when the scheme was involved. (Challis and Davies, p. 165)

Empowering carers; case management and Bexley ACE

One of the central problems facing many carers is that of activating and co-ordinating support services for their dependant and, more rarely, for themselves. The difficulties of co-ordination both within and between agencies are well attested, and have been the subject of a considerable organisational literature. Frequently, the person who experiences these difficulties most acutely is the carer who, together with the dependant, can sit at the centre of a complex net of support, both formal and informal. As a result, many carers are in effect the case managers for their dependant; indeed such a role is in a sense implicit in the aspect of responsibility that, as we have seen, is one of the key features of the carer role.

One scheme that has attempted to build on and systematise this case management role is that of the Bexley Community Care Scheme, which operates in conjunction with Bexley ACE, the Association for Carers for the Elderly. The Bexley Community Care Scheme originated in 1984 as an attempt to develop cost-effective alternatives to residential care. The carers of dependent people in the scheme formed themselves, with the help of a retired community worker, into the Association for Carers of the Elderly. The joint scheme has increasingly focused its activities on the carers of people with dementia. The work of the scheme is described, though sometimes rather evangelistically, by Foster and Maitland (1986), Chambers (1986), ACE (1986) and Maitland and Tutt (1987).

The community care scheme is a variant of the Kent model. It emphasises the use of individually recruited workers or helpers who are paid to provide flexible forms of support on the model of that provided by the informal sector. Where it differs from the classic Kent model is in the emphasis that is placed on the role of the carer. Here, the task of case manager is undertaken not by a paid worker, but by the carers themselves, who are encouraged to direct and coordinate support services for themselves and for their dependants. In order to do this, they receive support and help from the community care manager and from the expertise developed within ACE as a group.

Care is provided by three types of paid 'carer': neighbours, attendants and lodgers. Wherever possible, the family is helped to identify a suitable person living nearby who wants a job. These 'jobs' are flexibly defined and are open to negotiation between the carer and helper in the light of the particular needs of the dependent person.

The money to pay for care is generated from social security benefits and from charitable funds. The principal sources of assistance are the attendance allowance and, up until the recent social security changes, the domestic assistance allowance, a benefit that was payable to individuals in receipt of supplementary benefit. Obtaining these allowances, particularly the latter, could pose problems for carers, and part of the work of ACE involved developing advocacy skills among its members in order to press for such support in the individual cases. Bridging loans were also made available to carers while benefits were being negotiated.

Central to the philosophy of the scheme is the belief that people should have more control of their own lives; and there is a clear consumer emphasis in the approach. Maitland argues that the evidence from the progressive development of the scheme points clearly to the view that:

> 'paid neighbours' provide the 'best' and most consistent care and that most carers prefer to employ their own paid neighbour rather than use domiciliary services. (Foster and Maitland, 1986, p. 1)

From this, Maitland concludes:

> that the best way to empower carers is to give them cash rather than care – so long as that cash is combined with professional and peer support. (Maitland and Tutt, 1987)

The evaluation of the scheme suggests that the approach has been cost-effective at least from the view point of the local authority. Maitland and Tutt quote an average cost per client that compares favourably with other forms of community and residential support. The cost quoted is, however, the cost to the local authority and does not take fully into account the implications for the social security budget, or indeed for the carer. The scheme also benefits greatly from the active support of the local geriatrician, who is able to facilitate health service support to clients in the scheme.

The Bexley scheme is small and as yet has no imitators. But the issues it raises are important ones, and their implications extend beyond the particular scheme itself. What the Bexley scheme has attempted to do is to circumvent the paternalism and rigidity of formal service provision by injecting into it a consumer element. In this, money, and the power that money brings, are central. Maitland quotes Midwinter in his study of private domiciliary care where, commenting on consumer control, he remarks:

what is apparent is that the straightforward money transaction does, in many minds, strengthen and clarify that relation in favour of the customer. (Midwinter, 1986, p. 34)

In addition, the scheme has involved a blurring of the distinctions between 'formal' and 'informal' in such a way that the benefits and advantages of informal care – its quality, its flexibility, its personal character – can be mobilised by the formal sector. Maitland and Tutt believe that the scheme provides a model for how social services can resolve the dilemma of how to work with informal carers in ways that do not destroy the essential character of informal care.

A note of caution needs to be sounded. It is not clear that all carers will be able to undertake such a pro-active role. This applies in particular to the 'employment' of helpers, and to the negotiation with bureaucratic agencies. Both of these are activities in which considerable personal and class-related skills are required. It is also not clear how far the model meets the needs of those carers who are deeply immersed in the situation of caregiving. The approach builds on and develops a basic assumption of responsibility by the carer, and in this it reflects a reality. But there are circumstances in which this responsibility should not so easily be assumed and in which responsibility needs to be more widely shared. Part of the role of a case manager is to step back from the situation and assess the needs of the carer separate from that of the dependant. Asking carers to act as their own case managers makes that process harder, and denies to carers an independent assessment of their own situation. This is particularly important in the light of the evidence that suggests that carers often have low levels of consciousness concerning alternatives to their situation.

Such comments as applied to the Bexley scheme should not, however, disguise the limitations of formal services in this regard. Extensive counselling of the carer, support aimed at allowing the carer to consider the options fully, even proper recognition of the role of the carer in the dependants' situation may be part of the rhetoric of statutory service provision but they are far from being common features.

PART THREE

The implications for future research

The main part of this paper has reviewed the current state of knowledge in relation to the evaluation of the effectiveness of services for informal carers. From this, it will have become clear that, despite the considerable research development of the field that has taken place in recent years, knowledge concerning the relationship of services to informal care is still deficient. There are three broad areas in which this is the case. The first concerns policy and practice; the second the levels and patterns of provision for carers; and the last the effectiveness of services.

Policy and practice

Remarkably little is currently known of the response within agencies to carers. This is partly because the issue has only recently become a consciously articulated one, but it reflects also the uncertain and fragmented position that carers occupy within the social care system. The nature of this uncertain position has been outlined in the introduction and explored more fully elsewhere. One of the consequences of it is that little is known systematically about policy and practice as it has developed in relation to carers. Carers remain relatively invisible in the policy formulations of agencies, and the different roles that they play as resources, co-workers and co-clients further fragment our perception of them (Twigg, 1989).

Policy in this area remains obscure. Where it is articulated, it is usually in terms of bland statements concerning the need to support carers. Reference is sometimes made in this context to the burdens borne by carers, and to the importance of carers in supporting dependants who would otherwise require expensive formal help. But the implications of these two forms of statements are rarely spelt out. For example, how far is policy concerned with improving the quality of life of carers and, if so, in what relation to the quality of life of the dependant? That the two are often related should not obscure the existence of genuine conflicts of interest. Where resources are limited, they have to be targeted. But are the appropriate target groups, in relation to informal carers, those who are heavily stressed or those who might otherwise give up caregiving? The two may be related, but they are not co-existent. Is the prevention of institutiona- lisation the key outcome measure, and what are the implications for carers if it is? How far are services about preventing the erosion of caregiving? Is it appropriate sometimes to encourage and support carers in giving up caregiving? What is the attitude of the agency to substitution? In short, what *are* the appropriate aims of services in this field, and what are the relevant outcome domains that their evaluation should seek to measure? These questions are central to policy in relation to carers, but they have rarely received conscious articulation.

In the context of this lack of clearly spelt-out objectives, an understanding of 'policy' needs to be pursued at another level: that of the systematic practices and patterns of resource allocation prevalent in agencies. These could be said to constitute the operative or implicit policy. But once again, little research has as yet been undertaken in this field. There are, for example, no direct studies that examine the systematic assumptions made about carers by service providers or, perhaps more important, about particular types of carer or of caregiving relationships. Do practitioners have different expectations of male and female carers, and what are the conse- quences of these for service provision? How far is household structure used as a means of defining the nature of obligation? In what ways do the understandings that practitioners have of the nature of marriage affect their response to spouse-carers? Is the significance of independent living interpreted differently for younger as opposed to elderly dependants? Why do some carers appear to get more help than others? What factors trigger a response?

Much of this information is by its nature implicit, embedded in practice assumptions, in commonsense views formed in the culture of the office. The relatively undefined character of policy in this area means that these sorts of assumptions play a particularly important role in structuring services in relation to informal care. Gaining access to such implicit models poses the kinds of theoretical and methodological difficulties that are familiar from research into value systems or assumptive worlds more generally. Organisational studies have only recently begun to look at these important areas, and they have understandably concentrated on more visible client groups or subject areas than that of informal care. As a result, sophisticated accounts of operative policy in relation to carers are still lacking.

The logic of evaluation requires that the aims of an intervention be made clear and explicit. This is not always possible, and the example of informal care displays the difficulties that evaluation studies can encounter in these areas. For evaluation to proceed, some under-standing must be gained of the aims of the intervention which must be made open to description and analysis. Primary research on the implicit policy structures of agencies, and of different actors within agencies, is therefore essential as part of the attempt to evaluate the effectiveness of different services.

Just as front-line policy, implicit and otherwise, remains little explored, so does the organisational framework of services. What are the principal models of service provision for carers? How far, indeed, can such coherent models be said to have emerged?

Little research has been undertaken in this field, and the picture remains very fragmented. There is information about individual initiatives; for example, in the London Borough of Sutton where a development officer was appointed to research, co-ordinate and establish services across health and social services boundaries (Alderman, 1987; Benson, 1987; Pinchin, 1987). In other authorities, development officers or specialist workers for the elderly or for younger physically disabled people have been given the additional brief of developing policy and services in relation to carers, or at least of raising their profile among service providers. The activities of the Birmingham Special Action Project have been particularly notable (Jowell et al., 1987; Birmingham Special Action Project, nd). In other localities, for example, Newcastle, support for carers has been the subject of development and review as part of joint planning (Newcastle SSD, 1987). In other authorities, review has taken the form of concentrating on a particular service need of carers like respite care or information.

As yet, no attempt has been made to draw together or review these different forms of response. There is no systematic evidence on emerging practice and policy. As well as information about actual services, primary research is also needed into the different models of service provision and into their strategic policy aims.

It is important again to stress that this information is not only of interest in itself, but plays a crucial part in the evaluation of the effectiveness of services. It is not possible to evaluate services in support of carers where the basic information on the policy and practice is absent. What counts as a service here? To whom is it delivered? What is the organisational structure? How do services relate to one another? Most fundamentally, what are their aims? Understanding the answer to these questions is basic to the setting up of any adequate evaluation of the effectiveness of services.

The levels and patterns of provision

The second major area where information is needed concerns the extent of provision for carers. Part of the problem relates to the difficulty, referred to at the start of this review, in defining what counts a service for carers. Carers are not primarily clients or patients, and, failing to be such, rarely feature in statistics concerning service provision. We have noted, at a number of points in the review, the importance of standard statutory services in the support of carers. Systematic information about the extent of the use of such services in the support of carers is almost totally lacking. We have some information about changes in, for example, the allocation rules or practices of the home help service, but little exact information on the number or proportion of cases in which support for carers has been one of the reasons for the allocation. A similar point could be made in relation to day care. These are services known to be provided for carers, yet the extent of provision is very unclear.

Considerable primary research would be needed to uncover such patterns, let alone to quantify them. A recent attempt to establish the extent of provision for carers by Webb et al., for the Co-operative Women's Guild illustrates many of the conceptual and methodological problems that can arise. *People Who Care* is a report of a survey sent to health authorities and social service departments in England and Wales (Webb, Paskin and King, 1987). The questionnaire asked whether there was any specific provision for carers organised directly by the authority or indirectly on its behalf by the voluntary sector. Some 385 'schemes' were identified. The report describes the mean total per health authority as 2.1 and per social service department as 3.0, with considerable variation in the frequency distribution. The publicity that accompanied the launching of the report emphasised how 26 per cent of health authorities and 14 per cent of social service departments reported that they had no schemes for carers.

Difficulties arise, however, when one considers the nature of the answers. The questionnaire asked widely about 'provision for carers'. It appears from the accounts of the main functions of the schemes and from the way the research is written up, that the majority of answers refer to specifically carer-focused projects. Some 16 authorities, however, mentioned, in relation to carer provisions the home help service. While it is not possible to get behind the coding of the types of scheme, it appears that the answers reflected in some degree the complex and often ambiguous character of what can be defined as a service supporting carers. But it is hard to be confident that the report reflected this systematically, or that the statement that an area has no services in support of carers adequately represents the realities of provision.

If we confine the subject narrowly to those services that have an overtly carer focus, there is better understanding of the structure and content of services. Information on the extent of services is still very limited. Much of our knowledge derives from accounts of or evaluations of small-scale innovative schemes, and indeed this review has drawn heavily on such literature. It remains unclear how far such schemes are typical. The interest in them may result in a false impression of their frequency and geographical spread.

There have been some directories of initiatives, for example, that produced by the Social Work Service Development Group as part of their carer support initiative, *Fifty Styles of Caring* (DHSS, 1984), or the *Directory* produced over a number of years by Age Concern England (Cloke, 1982, 1983, 1985). These list various carer-related initiatives and schemes, but they do not attempt to provide a comprehensive sweep. *People Who Care* does come nearer to that, but the response rates were relatively low (53.5 per cent for health authorities and 46.5 per cent for social service departments) and there were the problems in methodology referred to above.

Where local surveys have been undertaken, for example, that of Moore and Green (1985) which reviewed the contribution of the voluntary sector to the support of carers in the Yorkshire and Humberside region, it appears that services are in fact very local, patchy and far from comprehensively available. Moore and Green comment in particular on the disappointingly small numbers of carers who are being helped by such schemes, and this point applies more widely than to just the voluntary sector. Anecdotal evidence from the carer associations and pressure groups suggest that carers frequently find that the services described and recommended to them in the literature are unavailable locally, or at least unavailable to *them*. The problem appears to be one of both the actual existence of services locally and of their capacity.

The area is one, furthermore, that is particularly prone to tokenism. Carers have of late been a fashionable subject. It can be tempting for authority members and chief officers to wish to be seen to be 'doing something for carers', even if that something is simply providing literature or setting up a research project. Such activities are useful, but they are inevitably limited in their impact. Small-scale support schemes that quickly 'silt up' with their initial clients can similarly be seen as performing a political function that is out of proportion to their overall impact on the problem.

There is no well-based systematic information about the incidence levels and patterns of support services and facilities. Basic research is still needed into the extent of provision. How many schemes are there, and how are they spread geographically? Does extent of provision reflect or follow other patterns of provision? How many people are catered for by these schemes, and at what intensity? What is their capacity to take on new people? How far are schemes supporting clients who were recruited early in the life of the project, with little room for new people? What forms of rationing or service allocation do they operate? Who controls access? What is a typical package of provision? What could one reasonably expect to encounter in any particular area?

Quite basic information is needed on these and other questions before an adequate account of the extent of provision for informal carers can be constructed. Without such an account it is impossible to get behind the rhetoric and determine whether support services are in reality available to carers. The absence of such an account is a major limitation in our understanding of the current situation.

The ramifications of this lack of knowledge have consequences that relate to the fields of policy and service development. So long as basic information about 'average' or 'typical' levels of provision is unavailable, development along the lines of performance indicators or of other prescriptive accounts of service provision is seriously inhibited. These approaches frequently draw upon average levels of provision in order to construct normative target levels. Such approaches have their own problems and limitations. They are open to the criticisms that have been made of, for example, bed norms in the health service: norms constructed around average provision have no necessary relationship to appropriate provision. And these problems may be compounded in the case of carer support by historically low levels of provision. Such 'average' or 'typical' data does provide some form of yardstick against which local provision might be judged. Any attempt to operationalise the approach any further is, however, hampered by the lack of information.

The effectiveness of services

The bulk of this review has been concerned with research that attempts to evaluate the effectiveness of services in support of carers. As we commented in the introduction, little such work has, until recently, been undertaken, and within this, research based on a rigorous or sophisticated evaluative methodology is still comparatively rare. As a result, information about the impact and effectiveness of services is far from comprehensive, and primary research is still needed.

Certain areas have in particular received insufficient attention. Long-established mainstream services whose principal target groups are the dependants rather than the carers have been poorly researched, at least from the perspective of carer support; yet, as we have noted, there is evidence that these services are among the most important for carers.

Similarly, there is almost no basic information, let alone evaluation, of the impact of services whose involvement with the carer is indirect. This applies in particular to medical services where the focus is very much on the patient and where the consequences of action for the carer are often only dimly perceived. These comments apply in particular to acute and hospital-based medicine.

A third area that has received insufficient attention has been the voluntary sector, where the reliance on volunteer labour in some projects has perhaps inhibited a systematic review of their effectiveness. This is much less the case where the projects have required outside funding to finance their operation, and there has been a recent plethora of publications on self evaluation in the voluntary sector. There can, however, be problems with the objectivity of such evaluations.

Evaluation, particularly outcome evaluation, requires control over the research situation. As a result, it is not surprising that those evaluations that have adopted a more rigorous methodology have tended to focus on particular discrete services, ideally based in an institutional setting. Services where the input is relatively fluid and complex, or where there is no single institutional setting, pose problems for evaluation, and they have correspondingly been less well researched. However, for informal carers supporting people who live in the community, these are precisely the sorts of service that are likely to be among the most significant.

Future evaluation work, as well as needing to concentrate on particular areas of services, needs to develop more refined analysis of the differential impact of service provision. This would involve exploring at greater levels of sophistication the ways in which factors like, for example, stress are mediated through particular features of the situation or characteristics of the carer. This would mean going beyond blanket statements that, for example, behavioural problems are associated with stress in the carer or the institutionalisation of the dependant, to explore for what sorts of people and in what sorts of situation this is the case. In a similar way, research needs to be undertaken to pursue the evidence that has begun to emerge about the differential impact of services on particular groups of carer. Who is most helped by respite care? For what sorts of carer is a home help useful?

As yet, the data available is relatively crude or unsystematic. Further research is needed, both at the level of large-scale, statistically-based studies and at the level of more detailed qualitative work, before these associations can be understood.

The implications of more refined understanding of this type are two-fold. At the simplest level, it can be used to improve practice, providing information that can alert practitioners to particular constellations of difficulty and to the potential impact of services on these. Information of this type is particularly useful in relation to informal care where there is some evidence of a reluctance on behalf of the carer to ask for or perhaps accept support services. Refined data on sources of stress and patterns of impact can provide practitioners and service providers with useful and objectively derived checklists for making assessments and referrals.

The second way such data can be used is as part of the overall planning of services. Policy makers and service planners need to know what sorts of services 'work' in order to make appropriate decisions about resources and how they are to be used. At issue here is not simply the question of whether a service has a beneficial effect, but whether that effect is greater or less when compared with other forms of support. How should service planners best use their resources to support informal care? Here, inevitably, the issue of cost enters the debate, for these are questions that are essentially those of value for money. It is not simply the differential impact of services that matter, but the ratio of these to their cost. How do hours of home help support compare with day care? What is the comparison to be made between intensive domiciliary support and forms of phased respite care?

These questions are implicit in the policy debates, but attempts to operationalise them within research are as yet in their infancy. Health economists have, perhaps, developed furthest these cost-effectiveness approaches within the evaluation of social and health care. The work in relation to global quality of life measures – QALYS, or quality adjusted life years – used in combination with cost estimates to measure the cost-effectiveness of different health care interventions is perhaps the best known example of such an approach. The work of the PSSRU has also gone some of the way towards the development of integrated, comparative measures of cost and benefit in the fields of social and long-term care (Davies and Challis, 1986).

There is not sufficient room in a review of this scope to outline the implications and problems of these more sophisticated approaches, and we have discussed elsewhere some of the difficulties that arise from attempting to apply such approaches to the support of informal carers (Twigg, 1988a). In noting that these approaches are as yet in their infancy, we do not want to suggest that the task is an easy or even an achievable one. It is important to emphasise here that the problems are not simply empirical or even methodological in character. They relate as much to policy itself, both in its content and its form, and as such they raise more deeply entrenched philosophical and political issues. In order to be able to develop these cost-effectiveness questions, a series of further questions need to be explored and answered. For example, how are intersubjective comparisons to be made? What is the 'worth' of one subjective state as against another? How feasible is it to construct a single utility measure against which to judge the impact of services? How could this be made to be intersubjectively valid? In what senses are individuals to be treated equally: for example, in terms of final outcome states, or in terms of the ratio of the cost of inputs to the level of outputs? How do we cope with the marked disequities between individuals in terms of social and cultural disadvantage? How would units of benefit be cross-related to units of cost? How far does the market provide evidence of these forms of value? How far is there any coherence in such judgements? How does one avoid the impact of differential income levels or should these in fact be allowed to affect the judgements?

At the moment, policy is simply not constructed in such a way as to provide answers to such questions and, indeed, given its complex political character, it is unlikely easily to become so.

Conclusion

This review has taken as its subject the evaluation of support to informal carers. From this material, certain broad conclusions emerge.

The first concerns the impact of those services that are currently provided. Earlier comments drawing attention to the relative lack of hard evaluative evidence concerning the impact of services should not be taken as suggesting any generally negative conclusion as to the overall impact of services. The trend of the evidence is quite clear: services do help to sustain carers, both in the sense of relieving strain and in enabling carers to continue to give care. Services can play an important, even vital, role in the lives of many carers. There is ample testimony from carers to this effect. In addition, there is 'objective' evidence that shows that services can reduce levels of stress and prevent the institutionalisation of the dependent person.

Beyond this, the picture becomes less clear. Exact evidence of the impact and effectiveness of different forms of provision is still largely lacking. Few, if any, evaluation studies have tackled the comparison of different forms of provision, and the amorphous character of 'provision' in this area makes such studies extremely difficult to mount.

The generally positive assessment of support services that we have noted must, however, be seen in conjunction with the second broad conclusion. This emerges less from the literature directly reviewed here than from the general carer literature, and it concerns the relative lack of support services for carers. There is now ample evidence as to the patchy and uncertain nature of carer support. Simply obtaining help can be a major problem; one compounded by lack of knowledge and by some of the other forms of indirect rationing operating with the system. The simple absence of services can be as significant to carers as their differential impact.

This relative lack of support services in turn affects the evaluation of the differential effectiveness of services. Few carers have received or been offered a variety of support packages sufficient to enable them to express a view as to their relative acceptability or effectiveness. One of the difficulties of asking carers about the effectiveness of support is that so many carers have little or no experience of services to discuss. Their comments, where they have received services, are often limited to a grateful account.

The third broad conclusion relates less to a particular substantive finding than to a general pattern of complexity. One of the emerging themes within the literature concerns the differential impact and acceptability of services on different sorts of carer. This review has chosen to look across client groups, and concentrate on a concept of carer per se. But perhaps as important as the unity of the carer experience is its structured diversity. Caregiving is embedded in social relations, and we should not be surprised to find that the character of those social relations strongly affect the potential role of services in the carer's life. There are significant differences, for example, in the meaning of caring for a young disabled spouse, compared with the meaning of caring for an elderly parent-in-law.

These differences affect the impact and acceptability of different forms of support service. Caregiving is embedded in gender relations and, again, we should not be surprised to find that services are experienced differently by men and women. The pattern is a complex one in which a variety of factors are important.

The fourth of these broad conclusions relates to policy itself; above all, to the uncertainty of policy in the field. This uncertainty relates both to the lack of knowledge of policy as it is currently operated by front-line practitioners, and to the uncertainty of policy-making bodies themselves as to exactly what their relations with carers are and should be. These uncertainties in their turn affect the evaluation literature, and lead to a lack of clarity within it. Determining appropriate outcome measures in relation to carers has as yet received little developed attention. The next stage of research in relation to carers must therefore attempt to engage with these difficulties and take forward the debate concerning the appropriate treatment of carers within the social care system.

Bibliography

ABBOT, B. (1983) 'CSV independent living scheme.' *Contact*, Spring, pp 47–9.

ACE, Bexley (1986) *Carers Voice*, May, p 1.

ALDERMAN, Charlotte (1987) 'Formal back up for informal carers.' *Nursing Times*, 83, 17 June, pp 51–3.

ALLEN, G. (1983) 'Informal networks of care: issues raised by Barclay.' *British Journal of Social Work*, 13, pp 1–12.

ALLEN, I. (1983) *Short-Stay Residential Care for the Elderly*. London: Policy Studies Institute.

ALZHEIMER'S DISEASE SOCIETY, (1984) *Caring for the Person with Dementia: A Guide for Families and Other Carers*. London: ADS.

ARBER, Sara, GILBERT, Nigel and EVANDROU, Maria, (1988) 'Gender, household composition and receipt of domiciliary services by the elderly disabled.' *Journal of Social Policy*, 17, 2, pp 153–175.

BADGER, F. CAMERON, E. and EVERS, H. (forthcoming) 'The nursing auxiliary service and care of elderly patients.' *Journal of Advanced Nursing*.

BALDWIN, S. and TWIGG, J. (1990) 'Women and community care: reflections on a debate'. In Maclean, M and Groves, D (eds) *Womens Issues in Social Policy*. London: Routledge.

BEBBINGTON, A. C., CHARNLEY, H., DAVIES, B. P., FERLIE, E. B., HUGHES, M. D. and TWIGG, J. (1986) *The Domiciliary Care Project: Meeting the Needs of the Elderly – Interim Report*. Canterbury: PSSRU.

BENSON, Sue (1987) 'Caring for the carers.' *Community Care*, 11 June, pp 25–7.

BERNARD, M. (1984) 'Voluntary care for the elderly mentally infirm and their relatives: a British example.' *Gerontologist*, 24(2), pp 116–19.

BIEGEL, D. E., SHORE, B. K. and GORDON, E. (1984) *Building Support Networks for the Elderly*. London: Sage.

BILLINGTON, J. (1987) 'Looking for new carers.' *Community Care*, 12 Feb, p 1.

BIRMINGHAM SPECIAL ACTION PROJECT (n.d) *Newsletter*, 1–6.

BOLDY, Duncan and KUH, Diana (1984) 'Short term care for elderly in residential homes: a research note.' *British Journal of Social Work*, 14, pp 173–5.

BONNY, S. (1984) *Who Cares in Southwark?* Rochester: Association of Carers.

BONSTELLE, S. J. (1980) 'Home care of aged stroke persons: family caregivers views.' Cleveland, Ohio, Case Western Reserve University, MSc. Thesis.

BOWLING, A. (1984) 'Caring for the elderly widowed – the burden of their supporters.' *British Journal of Social Work*, 14, pp 435–55.

BRIGGS, A. and OLIVER, J. (eds) (1985) *Caring: Experiences of Looking After Disabled Relatives*. London: Routledge.

BRISTOW A. K. (1981) *Crossroads Care Attendant Scheme*. Rugby: Association of Crossroads Care Attendant Schemes.

BRISTOW, A. K. (1986) *Cause for Concern: A Study of People Who Have the Ultimate Responsibility for Caring for a Severely Disabled and/or Elderly Person Living at Home*. Rugby: Association of Crossroads Care Attendant Schemes.

BRISTOW, A. K. and BRENIG-JONES, J. (1984) *An Appraisal of the Wirral Crossroads Care Attendant Scheme*. Rugby: Association of Crossroads Care Attendant Schemes.

BROOK, Peter and JESTICE Sue (1986) 'Relief for the demented and their relatives.' *Geriatric Medicine*, June, pp 31–6.

BRUNSWICK (1986) 'Carers Support Group: Report and Plan for Brunswick Patch'. Brighton: Sussex Social Services Department.

CANTOR, M. (1983) 'Strain among caregivers: a study of experience in the US.' *Gerontologist*, 23(6). pp 597–603.

CAMERON, E., BADGER, F., EVERS, H. and ATKIN, K. (1989) 'Black Old Women and Health Carers.' In Jeffreys, M.(ed) *Growing Old in the Twentieth Century*. London: Routledge.

CARTER, Jan (1981) *Day Services for Adults: Somewhere To Go*. London: Allen and Unwin.

CECIL, Rosanne, OFFER, John and ST. LEGER, Fred (1987) *Informal Welfare: A Sociological Study of Care in Northern Ireland*. Aldershot: Gower.

CHALLIS, D., LUCKETT, R. and CHESSUM, R. (1983) 'A new life at home.' *Community Care*, March 24, pp 21–3.

CHALLIS, D. and DAVIES, B. P. (1986) *Case Management in Community Care: An Evaluated Experiment in the Home Care of the Elderly*. Aldershot: Gower.

CHAMBERS, Peter (1986) 'Paid neighbours improve care for frail elderly.' *Geriatric Medicine*, November, pp 42–5.

CLOKE, C. (ed) (1983) *Caring for the Carers: A Directory of Initiatives*, second ed. Mitcham: Age Concern.

COOPER, M. (1985) *Hard-Won Reality: An Evaluation of the Essex Crossroads Care Attendant Schemes*. Braintree: Essex Social Services.

COOPER, M. (1986) 'On the Right Road.' *Community Care*, 14 August, p 24-5.

COWEN, Alison and JOHNSON, Micky (1985) *In Safe Hands: Home Care Relief Scheme: Report 1981–85*. York: Age Concern.

CREEK, G., MOORE, M., OLIVER, M., SALISBURY, V., SILVER, J. and ZARB, G. (1987) *Personal and Social Implications of Spinal Cord Injury: A Retrospective Study*. London: Thames Polytechnic.

CRINE, Alistair (1983) 'Two-way squeeze.' *Community Care*, 24 March, pp 14–15.

CROSBY, C., COPELAND, J. R. M., EL ASSRA, A. and STEVENSON, R. C. (1983) *The Intensive Domiciliary Care Scheme for Elderly Mentally Ill People: A Second Report*. Liverpool: University of Liverpool.

CROSBY, C., COPELAND, J. R. M., EL ASSRA, A. and STEVENSON, R. C. (1986) *The Liverpool Intensive Domiciliary Care Scheme for Elderly Mentally Ill People, 1981–1986*. Liverpool: University of Liverpool.

CROSBY, Ian (1985) 'Family placement for older people: a new approach to caring for older people.' *Australian Social Work*, 38(2), June 26, pp 26–30.

CROSSMAN, L., LONDON, C. and BARRY, C. (1981) 'Older women caring for disabled spouses: a model for supportive services.' *Gerontologist*, 21(5), pp 464–70.

CROSSROADS CARE ATTENDANT SCHEMES (1987) *Crossroads News*, Autumn 32.

CROSSTHWAITE, Alan (1989) *The Greenwich community care attendant scheme: an evaluation*. London: Directorate of Social Services, Borough of Greenwich.

DALLEY, Gillian (1983) 'Ideologies of care: a feminist contribution to the debate.' *Critical Social Policy*, pp 72–81.

DALLEY, Gillian (1988) *Ideologies of Caring: Rethinking Community and Collectivism*. London: Macmillan.

DANT, Tim (1988) 'Old, poor and at home: social security and elderly people in the community.' In Baldwin, S., Parker, G and Walker, R. (eds), *Social Security and Community Care*. Aldershot: Avebury.

DAVIES, B. P., and BEBBINGTON, A. C. (1983) 'Equity and efficiency in the allocation of personal social services.' *Journal of Social Policy*, 12, pp 309–29.

DAVIES, B. P. and CHALLIS, D. (1986) *Matching Resources to Needs in Community Care*. Aldershot: Gower.

DAVIES, Mary D. (1989) *Doctors, Carers and General Practice*. London: MSD Foundation.

DEPARTMENT OF HEALTH AND SOCIAL SECURITY (1984) *Fifty Styles of Caring: Models of Practice for Planners and Practitioners*. London: SSI, DHSS.

DONALDSON, C., CLARK, K., GREGNON, B., BACKHOUSE, M., and PRAGNALL, C. (1988) *Evaluation of a Family Support Unit for Elderly Mentally Infirm People and their Carers*. Newcastle: Health Care Research Unit, University of Newcastle on Tyne.

DOYLE, B. and HUNT, P. (1985) 'Day care for the elderly.' *Health and Social Service Journal*. April 11, pp 448–9.

EVANS, Neil, KENDALL, Ian, LOVELOCK, Robin and POWELL, Jackie (1986) *Something to Look Forward To: An Evaluation of a Travelling Day Hospital for Elderly Mentally Ill People*. Portsmouth: SSRIU.

FADDEN, G., BEBBINGTON, P. and KUIPERS, L. (1987) 'The burden of care: the impact of functional psychiatric illness on the patient's family.' *British Journal of Psychiatry*, 150, pp 285–92.

FARNSWORTH, S. (1986) *The Evaluation of the Cheltenham and District Crossroads Care Attendant Scheme: The Results of the Questionnaires to Carers*. Gloucester: Gloucester County Council.

FARRIES, John (1985) 'Giving the carers a much needed break.' *Health and Social Services Journal*, 8 Aug, pp 986–7.

FENGLER, A. P. and GOODRICH, N. (1979) 'The wives of elderly disabled: the hidden patients.' *Gerontologist*, 19, 2, pp 175-83.

FENNELL, G., EMERSON, A. R., SIDELL, M. and HAGUE, A. (1981) *Day Centres for the Elderly in East Anglia*. Norwich: Centre for East Anglian Studies.

FERLIE, Ewan (forthcoming), 'Organisational variation and community services.' In Bebbington, A., Davies, B. P., Charnley, H., Ferlie, E., Hughes, M., Twigg J., Needs, Resources and Outcomes in Community Based Care A Comparative Study of Services for the Elderly. Aldershot: Gower.

FINCH, J. (1984), 'Community care: developing non-sexist alternatives.' *Critical Social Policy*, 9, pp 6–18.

FINCH, Janet (1987) 'Whose Responsibility? Women and the future of family care.' In Allen, I., Wicks, M., Finch, J., Leat D. (eds) *Informal Care Tomorrow*. London: PSI.

FINCH, J. (1989) *Family Obligations and Social Change*. Cambridge: Polity Press.

FINCH, J., and GROVES, D. (eds) (1983) *A Labour of Love: Women, Work and Caring*. London: Routledge.

FORSTER, Annette (1985) 'How to start a support group for relatives looking after a dementia sufferer.' In Osborne, A. (ed) *Reaching Out to Dementia Sufferers and Their Carers*. Edinburgh: Age Concern Scotland.

FOSTER, Carol and MAITLAND, Nan (1986) 'Empowering carers: Bexley ACE, the Bexley community care scheme and the health service.' Unpublished paper, Bexley Social Services.

FRANK, L. (1984) 'Respite care for the elderly: some organisational and planning issues.' *Proceedings of Australian Association of Gerontology*, 19th Conference, Sydney, 1984

FROLAND, C. (1981) 'Formal and informal care: discontinuities in a continuum.' *Social Service Review*, S4 pp 572–87.

FROLAND, C., PANCOAST, D., CHAPMAN, N. and KIMBOKO, P. (1981) *Helping Networks and Human Services*. London: Sage.

FULLER, J., WARD, E., EVANS, A., MASSAM, K. and GARDENER, A. (1979) 'Dementia: supportive groups for relatives.' *BMJ*, 23 June, pp 1684–5.

GILHOOLY, M. (1982) 'Social aspects of senile dementia.' In Taylor, R. and Gilmore, A. (eds), *Current Trends in British Gerontology*. Aldershot: Gower.

GILHOOLY, M. (1984) 'The impact of caregiving on caregivers: factors associated with the psychological well-being of people supporting a dementing relative in the community.' *B. J. of Medical Psychology*,57, pp 35–43.

GILLEARD, C. J. (1984) *Living with Dementia: Community Care of the Elderly Mentally Infirm*. London: Croom Helm.

GILLEARD, C. J., GILLEARD, E., GLEDHILL, K. and WHITTICK, J. (1984a) 'Caring for the elderly mentally infirm at home: a survey of supporters.' *J. of Epid. & Community Health*, 38, pp 319–24.

GILLEARD, C. J., GILLEARD, E. and WHITTICK, J. E. (1984b) 'Impact of psychogeriatric day hospital care on the patients family.' *B. J. Psychiatry*, 145, pp 487–92.

GLENDINNING, C. (1983) *Unshared Care: Parents and their Disabled Children*. London: Routledge.

GLENDINNING, C. (1987) *The Financial Circumstances of Informal Carers: Interim Report*. York: Social Policy Research Unit Discussion Paper.

GLENDINNING, C. (1989) *The Financial Circumstances of Informal Carers: Final Report*. York: Social Policy Research Unit Discussion Paper.

GLOSSER, G. and WEXLER, D. (1985) 'Participants evaluation of educational/ support groups for families of patients with Alzheimer's Disease and other dementias.' *Gerontologist*, 25(3), pp 232–6.

GOLDSTEIN, Vida, REGNERY, Gretchen and WELLIN, Edward (1981) 'Caretaker role fatigue.' *Nursing Outlook*, January, pp 24–30.

GRAHAM, Hilary (1983) 'Caring: labour of love.' In Finch, J. and Groves, D. (eds), *A Labour of Love: Women, Work and Caring*. London: Routledge.

GRANT, G. (1986) 'Older carers, interdependence and the care of mentally handicapped adults.' *Ageing and Society*, 6, 3, pp 333–51.

GREEN, Hazel (1988) *Informal Carers*. London: OPCS.

GREENE, J. G. and TIMBURY, G. C. (1979) 'A geriatric psychiatry day hospital service: a five year review.' *Age and Ageing*, 8, pp 49–53.

HARPUR, S. and LUND, D. (1987) 'Some correlates of burden for caregivers of senile dementia patients.' Paper presented to 1987 Brighton Conference: Ageing Well.

HARTFORD, M. E. and PARSONS, R. (1982) 'Uses of groups with relatives of dependent older adults.' *Social Work with Groups*, 5(2), pp 77–87.

HASSELKUS, B. R. and BROWN, M. (1983) 'Respite care for community elderly.' *American Journal of Occupational Therapy*, 37, 2, pp 83–8.

HAUSMAN, C. P. (1979) 'Short-term counselling groups for people with elderly parents.' *Gerontologist*, 19, 1, pp 102–7.

HEDLEY, R. and NORMAN, A. (1982), *Home Help: Key Issues in Service Provision*. London: Centre for Policy on Ageing.

HENDERSON, J. (1987) 'Conceptualisation of informal care: An analysis of community care policies based upon the perceptions of informal carers of elderly dependent women.' PhD thesis presented at the University of Bradford.

HERBERT, Y., WILLISON, J. and ZABORSKI, A. (1983) 'Strength in sadness.' *Social Work Today*, 18 Oct, pp 14–15.

HETTIARATCHY, P., and MANTHORPE, J. (forthcoming) 'Group psychotherapy supporting the carers of elderly mentally ill people.' In Jones, G. and Miesen, B. M. L. (eds) *Care Giving in Dementia*. London: Wiley.

HINRICHSEN, G. A., REVENSON, T. A. and SHINN, M. (1985) 'Does self-help help? An empirical investigation of scoliosis peer support group.' *J. of Social Issues*, 41, 1, pp 65–87.

HODGE, H. (1987) 'I'm gonna sit right down and...' *Health Service Journal*, 15 Jan, pp 64–5.

HOOYMAN, N., GONYEA, J. and MONTGOMERY, R. (1985) 'The impact of in-home services termination on family caregivers,' *Gerontologist*, 25, 2, pp 141–5.

HOPPER, C. and ROBERTS, J. (nd) *Care Attendant Schemes: Their Management and Organisation Care Attendant Schemes in Greater London. A Survey: The Redbridge Care Attendant Scheme: A Case Study.* London: GLAD.

JORDAN, B. (1987) 'Preliminary Study for the Carers' Charter.' Unpublished report to Kings Fund.

JOWELL, T., QUINN, L. and ELSON, B. (1987) 'Caring about carers.' In Twigg, J. (ed) *Evaluating Support to Informal Carers.* York: SPRU.

KEATING, J. and RICKETT, A. (1982) 'Bolton's short-term family placement scheme for elderly people.' *Social Work Service,* Winter, pp 46–50.

KEEGAN, M. (1984) 'A day centre for the elderly mentally infirm.' In Isaacs, B. and Evers, H. *Innovations in the Care of the Elderly.* London: Croom Helm.

KELSON, Nora (1985) *The Short-Term Care Project, Eastern Counties: Final Report to the Welfare Advisory Panel.* London: Parkinson's Disease Society.

KINGS FUND INFORMAL CARING PROGRAMME (1987) *Taking a Break: A Guide for People Caring at Home.* London: Kings Fund.

KOHNER, Nancy (1988) *Caring at Home.* Cambridge: National Extension College.

LEAT, Diana (1987) 'Informal care and respite care schemes: support or take over.' In Twigg, J. (ed) *Evaluating Support to Informal Carers.* York: Social Policy Research Unit.

LEAT, Diana and GAY, Pat (1987) *Paying for Care: A Study of Policy and Practice In Paid Care Schemes.* London: PSI.

LEVIN, E., SINCLAIR, I. and GORBACH, P. (1983) *The Supporters of Confused Elderly Persons at Home.* London: NISW.

LEVIN, E., SINCLAIR, I. and GORBACH, P. (1985) 'The effectiveness of the home help service with confused old people and their families.' *Research, Policy and Planning,* 3(2), pp 1–7.

LEWIS, Jane and MEREDITH, Barbara (1988) 'Daughters caring for mothers: the experience of caring and its implications for professional helpers.' *Ageing and Society,* 8, pp 1–22.

LEWIS, Jane and MEREDITH, Barbara (1988) *Daughters Who Care: Daughters Caring for Mothers at Home.* London: Routledge.

LITWAK, E. and KULIS, S. (1983) 'Changes in helping networks with changes in the health of old people: social policy and social theory.' In Spiro, S. E. and Yuchtman-Yaar, E. (eds) *Evaluating the Welfare State.* New York: Academic Press.

LLEWELYN, S. P. and HASLETT, A. V. J. (1986) 'Factors perceived as helpful by the members of self-help groups: an exploratory study,' *British Journal of Guidance and Counselling,* 14, 3, pp 252–62.

LODGE, B. and McREYNOLDS, S. (1983) *Quadruple Support for Dementia: Community Support for Mentally Infirm Elderly People in Hinckley, Leicestershire – a Multidiscipliniary Exercise.* Hinckley: Leicester SSD.

LOVELOCK, R. (1981) *...Friends In Deed: Three Care Attendant Schemes for the Younger Physically Disabled In Hampshire.* Portsmouth: SSRIU.

LOVELOCK, R. (1985) *Against the Tide: Approaches to the Domiciliary Support of Frail Elderly People In Hampshire.* Portsmouth: SSRIU.

MAITLAND, Nan and TUTT, Norman (1987) 'Bexley's trump card.' *Social Services Insight*, 18 September, pp 16–17.

MAY, David, McKEGANEY, Neil and FLOOD, Mary (1986) 'Extra hands or extra problems.' *Nursing Times*, 3 September, pp 35–8.

McKAY, B., NORTH, N. and MURRAY-SYKES, K. (1983) 'The effect on carers of hospital admission of the elderly.' *Nursing Times*, 30 Nov, pp 42–3.

McLACHLAN, S., SHEARD, D. and ANDERSON, K. (1985) 'Relatives' open evenings can help.' *Health and Social Services Journal*, 14 Nov, pp 1142–3.

MELVILLE, J. (1987) 'Taking care of the carers.' *New Society*, 10 July, p 24.

MIDWINTER, Eric (1986) *Caring for Cash*. London: Centre for Policy on Ageing.

MILLER, D. B., GULLE, N. and McCUE, F. (1986) 'The realities of respite for families, clients and sponsors.' *Gerontologist*, 26, pp 467–70.

MOORE, J. and THORNTON, P. (1981) *Voluntary Sector Relative Support Provision: Interim Report to SSRC*. Leeds: Department of Social Policy & Administration.

MOORE, J. and GREEN, J. M. (1985) 'The contribution of voluntary organisations to the support of caring relatives.' *Quarterly Journal of Social Affairs*, I, 2, pp 93–130.

MOORE, L. (1985) *Report of the Paid Sitting Service Pilot Scheme*. Bristol: SEMI.

MOORE, Liz (1985) 'Supporting relatives.' *Community Care*, 14 Nov, pp 21–2.

MORONEY, R. (1986) *Shared Responsibility: Families and Social Policy*. New York: Aldine.

MULLENDER, A. (1983) 'Someone to look after grandma.' *Community Care*, 15 Sept, pp 22–3.

MURPHY, E. (1985) 'Day care: who and what is it for?' *New Age*, 31, pp 7–9

MYKYTA, L. J., BOWLING, J. H., NELSON, D. A. and, LLOYD, E. J. (1976) 'Caring for relatives of stroke patients.' *Age and Ageing*, 5, pp 87–90.

NEWCASTLE CITY COUNCIL (1986) *Respite Family Care and Mental Handicap in Newcastle*. Newcastle: City of Newcastle Policy Services and Social Services Departments.

NEWCASTLE SOCIAL SERVICES DEPARTMENT (1986) *Respite Family Care and Mental Handicap In Newcastle: An Evaluation of the FACE and STOP Schemes*. Newcastle: SSD.

NEWCASTLE SOCIAL SERVICES DEPARTMENT (1987) *A Review of Carers Support In Newcastle 1986–87: Report of Joint Care Planning Team*. Newcastle: SSD.

NEWTON, S. (1981) 'A short-term boarding out scheme for the elderly.' *Social Work Service*, 26, pp 1–3.

NISSEL, M. and BONNERJEA, L. (1982) *Family Care of Handicapped Elderly: Who Pays?* London: PSI.

NORTH, S. (1985) 'Breaking point.' *Nursing Mirror*, 18 September, pp 42–3.

NORTH YORKSHIRE SOCIAL SERVICES DEPARTMENT (nd, 1986 and 1987) *Handbook for Carers*. Northallerton: SSD.

OLIVER, Mike (1988) 'Flexible services.' *Nursing Times*, 6 April, pp 25–31.

OSBORNE, P. (1981) 'Crossroads care for the carers.' *Geriatric Medicine*, May, pp 59–62.

OSBORNE, P. (1986) 'Preface.' In Bristow, A. K., *Cause for Concern*. Rugby: Association of Crossroads Care Attendant Schemes.

OSWIN, Maureen (1984) *They Keep Going Away: A Critical Study of Short-Term Residential Care Services for Children Who Are Mentally Handicapped*. London: King Edwards Hospital Fund for London.

PANCOAST, D. L. and COLLINS, A. H. (1976) *Natural Helping Networks*. London: Sage.

PANCOAST, D. L., PARKER, P. and FROLAND C. (eds) (1983) *Re-discovering Self-Help: Its Role in Social Care*. London: Sage.

PARKER, Gillian (1985: 2nd ed 1990) *With Due Care and Attention: A Review of Research on Informal Care*. London: Family Policy Studies Centre.

PARKER, Gillian (1989) *A Study of Non-Elderly Spouse Carers: Final Report*. York: Social Policy Research Unit Discussion Paper.

PARKER, R. (1981) 'Tending and social policy.' In Goldberg, E. M. and Hatch, S., *A New Look at the Personal Social Services*. London: PSI.

PERRING, C., TWIGG, J. and ATKIN, K. (1990) *Families Caring for People Diagnosed as Mentally Ill: the Literature Re-examined*. London: HMSO.

PINCHIN, Anne (1987) *Developing a Strategy for Respite Care: A Report from the Sutton Carers' Project of the London Borough of Sutton and the Merton and Sutton Health Authority*. Sutton: SSD.

QURESHI, H. and WALKER, A. (1989) *The Caring Relationship: Elderly People and Their Families*. Basingstoke: Macmillan.

RAMDAS, A. (1986) 'Getting it right: women carers of the frail elderly: an analysis of experiences and support service needs.' MA Thesis, University of York.

RICE, A. (1984) 'Desperate in Seaford.' *Community Care*, 13 Sept, pp 15–16.

RICHARDSON, A. and GOODMAN, M. (1983) *Self-Help and Social Care: Mutual Aid Organisations in Practice*. London: PSI.

RICHARDSON, A. (1983) 'English self-help: varied patterns and practices.' In Pancoast, D. L., Parker, P. and Froland, C. (eds), *Rediscovering Self-Help: Its Role in Social Care*. London: Sage.

RIMMER, L. and WICKS, M. (1983) 'The challenge of change: demographic trends, the family and social policy.' In Glennerster H. (ed), *The Future of the Welfare State*. London: Heinemann.

ROBINSON, B. and THURNHER, M. (1979) 'Taking care of aged parents: a family cycle transition.' *Gerontologist*, 19.

ROBINSON, Janice (1988) 'Support systems'. *Nursing Times*, 6 April, pp 30–1.

ROBINSON, Tim and LUSZCZAK, Peter (1986) 'The Rushcliffe blend.' *Community Care*, 8 May, pp 18–19.

SADDINGTON, N. (1984) 'Courses for carers.' *Nursing Times*, 12 Dec, pp 434.

SAFFORD, F. (1980) 'A program for families of the mentally impaired elderly.' *Gerontologist*, 20(6), pp 656–61.

SANDFORD, J. R. A. (1975) 'Tolerance of debility in elderly dependents by supporters at home: its significance for hospital practice.' *BMJ,3*, pp 471–3.

SCHARLACH, Andrew and FRENZEL, C. (1986) 'An evaluation of institution-based respite care.' *Gerontologist*, 26, 1, pp 77–81.

SCHMIDT, G. L. and KEYES, B. (1985) 'Group psychotherapy with family caregivers of demented patients.' *Gerontologist*, 25, pp 347–50.

SIMPSON, J. A. and TRAYNOR, J. (1987) *Ten Years of Family Placement for Older People: Report and Review*. Leeds: Department of Social Service.

SMITH, G. and CANTLEY, C. (1985) *Assessing Health Care: A Study in Organisational Evaluation*. Milton Keynes: OU.

SMITH, M. (1983) 'Finding the strength.' *Social Work Today*, 12 July, pp 16–17.

SMITH, M. (1986) *Durham Community Care Domiciliary Respite Care Scheme: Final Report*, Durham: Durham Community Care.

SNYDER, B. and KEEFE, K. (1985) 'The unmet needs of family caregivers for frail and disabled adults.' *Social Work in Health Care*, 10(3), pp 1–14.

SOCIAL SERVICES INSPECTORATE (1987a) *Care for a Change?: Inspection of Short-Term Care in the Personal Social Services*. London: SSI, DHSS.

SOCIAL SERVICES INSPECTORATE (1987b) *From Home Help to Home Care: An Analysis of Policy, Resourcing and Service Management*. London: SSI, DHSS.

SOCIAL SERVICES INSPECTORATE (1988) *Managing Policy Change in the Home Help Service*. London: SSI, DHSS.

SOUTHAMPTON MIND (1984) 'A sitting at home with grandma service.' *Health and Social Services Journal*, 5 July, pp 800–1.

STEPHENS, S. A. and CHRISTIANSON, J. B. (1986) *Informal Care of the Elderly*. Lexington: Lexington Books.

TESTER, Susan, (1989) 'Day care for elderly people,' *Social Work Today*, 2 Feb, pp 20–1.

THOMPSON, D. M. (1986) *'Calling all carers' survey: South Manchester. 1985–1986 Report*. Manchester: privately published.

THORNTON, P. and MOORE J. (1980) *The Placement of Elderly People in Private Households: An Analysis of Current Provision*. Leeds: Department of Social Policy University of Leeds.

THORNTON, P. (1989a) *Creating a Break: A Home Care Relief Scheme for Elderly People and Their Supporters*. Mitcham: Age Concern England.

THORNTON, P. (1989b) 'Caring with caution'. *Health Service Journal*, 10 August, pp 972–3.

TRISELIOTIS, V. (1985) *Time for Ourselves: Creating a Sitter Service*. Edinburgh: Scottish Council for Single Parents.

TWIGG, J. (ed) (1987) *Evaluating Support to Informal Carers: Papers Presented at a Conference Held in York, September 1987*. York: Social Policy Research Unit.

TWIGG, J. (1988a), 'Evaluating support to informal carers: some conceptual issues.' York: Social Policy Research Unit Discussion Paper.

TWIGG, J. (1988b) 'With carers in mind'. *CareLink*, Summer 1988, No. 5, p 7.

TWIGG, J. (1989) 'Models of carers: how do agencies conceptualise their relation with informal carers.' *Journal of Social Policy*, 18, I, pp 53–66.

TWIGG, J. (forthcoming) 'Personal care and the interface between the district nursing and home help services.' In Davies, B. P., Bebbington, A. C. and Charnley, H. *Resources, Needs and Outcomes in Community Based Care*. Aldershot: Gower

UNGERSON, Clare (1987) *Policy is Personal: Sex, Gender and Informal Care*. London: Tavistock.

WAERNESS, K. (1984) 'The rationality of caring'. *Economic and Industrial Democracy*, Vol. 5, pp 185–210.

WATSON, Carol (1983); 'Intermittant admission: an answer to home care?' *Therapy Weekly*, 4 August, p 4.

WATT, Glenda M. (1982) 'A family-oriented approach to community care for the elderly mentally infirm.' *Nursing Times*, September 15, pp 1545–8.

WEAVER, Tim, WILLCOCKS, Dianne and KELLAHER, Leonie (1985) *The Business of Care: A Study of Private Residential Homes for Old People*. London: CESSA, North London Polytechnic.

WEBB, Iris, PASKIN, Diane and KING, Sue (1987) *People Who Care: A Report on Carer Provision in England and Wales for the Co-operative Women's Guild*. London: Co-operative Womens Guild.

WICKS, M. (1982) 'Community care and elderly people.' In Walker A. (ed), *Community Care: the Family, the State and Social Policy*. Oxford: Blackwell.

WILLIAMS, E. and FRANCIS, S. (1988) 'Days of old.' *Insight*, 18 March, pp 21–3.

WILSON, E. (1982) 'Women, the "community" and the "family".' In Walker, A. (ed.), *Community Care: The Family, the State and Social Policy*. Oxford: Blackwell.

WILSON, J. (1986) *Self-Help Groups: Getting Started – Keeping Going*. London: Longmans.

WILSON, J. (1988) *Caring Together: Guidelines for Carers' Self-Help and Support Groups*, Cambridge: National Extension College.

WRIGHT, F. D. (1986) *Left to Care Alone*. Aldershot: Gower.

WRIGHT, K. (1987) *The Economics of Informal Care of the Elderly*. York: Centre for Health Economics, York.

ZARIT, S. H., REEVER, K. E and BACH-PETERSON, J. (1980) 'Relatives of impared elderly: correlates of feelings of burden.' *Gerontologist*, 20, 6, pp 649–55.

Index

Printed in the United Kingdom for HMSO.
Dd.299811, 8/94, C2, 3396/4, 5673, 296152.